Francis A. Schaeffer

GENESIS
IN SPACE & TIME

the flow of biblical history

co-published by

Regal Books, G/L Publications
Glendale, California, U.S.A.

InterVarsity Press
Downers Grove, Illinois 60515

InterVarsity Press is
the book publishing division
of Inter-Varsity
Christian Fellowship.

ISBN 0-87784-636-7

Library of Congress Catalog
Card Number: 72-78406

Printed in the United
States of America

books by Francis A. Schaeffer:

Escape from Reason
The God Who Is There
Death in the City
Pollution and the Death of Man, the Christian View of Ecology
The Church at the End of the 20th Century
The Mark of the Christian
The Church before the Watching World
True Spirituality
He Is There and He Is Not Silent
Basic Bible Studies
The New Super-Spirituality
Back to Freedom and Dignity

To all those who have made it possible to
publish these ten related books in the past five years.
I especially want to say thank you to James Sire
of the United States and David Winter of Britain
without whose understanding editorial work
on my manuscripts this would not have been possible.

contents

preface 9

chapter 1 creation 13

chapter 2 differentiation and the creation of man 35

chapter 3 God and his universe 57

chapter 4 the point of decision 71

chapter 5 the space-time fall and its results 89

chapter 6 the two humanities 109

chapter 7 Noah and the flood 127

chapter 8 from Noah to Babel to Abraham 149

appendix concerning the books by Francis and Edith Schaeffer 169

footnotes 172

The battle for a Christian understanding of the world is being waged on several fronts. Not the least of these is biblical study in general, and especially the question of how the opening chapters of the Bible are to be read. Modern writers commenting on the book of Genesis tend to treat the first eleven chapters as something other than history. For some this material is simply a Jewish myth, having no more historical validity for modern man than the Epic of Gilgamesh or the stories of Zeus. For others it forms a pre-scientific vision that no one who respects the results of scholarship can accept. Still others find the story symbolic but no more. Some accept the early chapters of Genesis as revelation in regard to an upper-story, religious truth, but allow any sense of truth in regard to history and the cosmos (science) to be lost.

How should these early chapters of Genesis be read? Are they historical and if so what value does their historicity have? In dealing with these questions, I wish to point out the tremendous value Genesis 1–11 has for modern man. In some ways these chapters are the most important ones in the Bible, for they put man in his cosmic setting and show him his peculiar uniqueness. They explain man's wonder and yet his flaw. Without a proper understanding of these chapters we have no answer to the problems of metaphysics, morals or epistemology, and furthermore, the   9 work of Christ becomes one more upper-story "religious" answer.

Although I have often made deliberate changes, I have used the King James Version throughout the book. Occasionally, where the American Standard Version (ASV) is helpful, I have quoted from it.

I would like to thank Professor Elmer Smick, a friend of many years, who read the manuscript and offered helpful suggestions. Any errors are certainly my own.

chapter 1

creation

The subject of this book is the flow of biblical history. The focal passage of Scripture is the first major section of Genesis (chapters 1–11) which traces the course of events from the creation of the universe to the calling forth of Abraham and the beginning of the history of Israel.

One of the hymns of Israel, Psalm 136, forms an excellent backdrop against which to see the unfolding of biblical history. It sets the conception of God as Creator in proper relation to man as creature and worshipper.

> O give thanks unto the LORD; for he is good:
>> for his mercy endureth for ever.
> O give thanks unto the God of gods:
>> for his mercy endureth for ever.
> O give thanks to the Lord of lords:
>> for his mercy endureth for ever.
> To him who alone doeth great wonders:
>> for his mercy endureth for ever. (vv. 1-4)

Psalm 136 thus begins with a three-fold doxology and then lists various reasons why we can praise God and why we are called upon to give thanks for his goodness. It is interesting that after giving a general reason for praise (that he "alone doeth great wonders") the psalmist directs our attention first to God's creative acts:

> To him that by wisdom made the heavens:
>> for his mercy endureth for ever.

> To him that stretched out the earth above the waters:
>> for his mercy endureth for ever.
> To him that made great lights:
>> for his mercy endureth for ever:
> The sun to rule by day:
>> for his mercy endureth for ever:
> The moon and stars to rule by night:
>> for his mercy endureth for ever. (vv. 5-9)

But immediately after expressing and developing the fact of God as Creator, the psalmist sweeps on to a second reason for praising God—the way God acted in history when the Jewish nation was captive in Egypt.

> To him that smote Egypt in their first born:
>> for his mercy endureth for ever:
> And brought out Israel from among them:
>> for his mercy endureth for ever: . . . (vv. 10-11)

The psalmist goes on to talk about the exodus, the dividing of the Red Sea, the overthrow of Pharaoh and the capture of the land of Canaan (vv. 12-21).

Then he turns to praise God for the way God is acting at the particular moment of space-time history in which this psalm was written:

> Even an heritage unto Israel his servant:
>> for his mercy endureth for ever.
> Who remembered us in our low estate:
>> for his mercy endureth for ever:
> And hath redeemed us from our enemies:
>> for his mercy endureth for ever.
> Who giveth food to all flesh:
>> for his mercy endureth for ever. (vv. 22-25)

Finally in the last verse, the psalmist writes in such a way that he speaks even for us at our own point in history and incites us to call upon God and praise him:

> O give thanks unto the God of heaven:
>> for his mercy endureth for ever. (v. 26)

So Psalm 136 brings us face to face with the biblical concept of creation as a fact of space-time history, for we find here a complete parallel between creation and other points of history: the space-timeness of history at the time of the Jewish captivity in Egypt, of the particular time in which the psalm itself was written and of our own time as we read the psalm today. The mentality of the whole Scripture, not just of this one psalm, is that creation is as historically real as the history of the Jews and our own present moment of time. Both the Old and the New Testaments deliberately root themselves back into the early chapters of Genesis, insisting that they are a record of historical events. What is the hermeneutical principle involved here? Surely the Bible itself gives it: The early chapters of Genesis are to be viewed completely as history —just as much so, let us say, as records concerning Abraham, David, Solomon or Jesus Christ.

In the Beginning

The opening verse of Genesis, "In the beginning God created the heavens and the earth," and the remainder of chapter 1 brings us immediately into a world of space and time. Space and time are like warp and woof. Their interwoven relationship is history. Thus the opening sentence of Genesis and the structure of what follows emphasize that we are dealing here with history just as much as if we talked about ourselves at this moment at a particular point of time in a particular geographic place.

In saying this, of course, we are considering the Jewish concept of truth. Many people today think that the Jewish concept is rather close to the modern one—that truth is irrational. But this is not the case. In fact, when we examine the Greek concept of truth in relationship to the Jewish concept, we find this difference. Many of the Greek philosophers saw truth as the expression of a nicely-balanced metaphysical system, rather like a mobile. That is, as long as the system balanced, it could be left alone and considered true. The Jewish concept is the opposite of this. First, it is completely opposite from the modern concept of truth because it is concerned with that which is open to discussion, open to rationality, and is not just an existential leap. Here it is like the Greek notion. And yet, it differs from and is deeper than the Greek concept because it is rooted in that which is historical. For example, we find Moses insisting, "You saw! You heard!" In Deuteronomy 4 and 5, just before he died, Moses reminded the Jews who stood before him that when they were young they themselves had seen and heard what had occurred at Sinai, that is, in space-time history. Their parents had died in the wilderness, but they, the children, had seen and heard in history. Joshua spoke the same way a bit later in Joshua 23:3 ff. As a matter of fact we have an exact parallel in these and other Old Testament passages to John's explanation of why he wrote the Gospel of John. "And many other space-time proofs [that is what the idea is here] truly did Jesus in the presence of his disciples, which are not written in this book: But these are written, that ye might believe that Jesus is the Christ, the Son of God; and that believing ye might have life through his name" (John 20:30-31).

As we deal with the Jewish writings in the Bible and with the book of Genesis in particular, we must not understand it solely in Greek terms nor, certainly, in terms of an existential leap. Instead, we have an insistence upon history, truth that is rooted in space and time.

Before the Beginning
Although Genesis begins, "In the beginning," that does not mean that there was not anything before that. In John

17:24, Jesus prays to God the Father, saying, "Thou

lovedst me before the foundation of the world." Jesus says that God the Father loved him prior to the creation of all else. And in John 17:5 Jesus asks the Father to glorify him, Jesus himself, "with the glory which I had with thee before the world was."

There is, therefore, something that reaches back into eternity—back before the phrase "in the beginning." Christ existed, and he had glory with the Father, and he was loved by the Father before "in the beginning." In Ephesians 1:4 we read, ". . . he [God] hath chosen us in him [Christ] before the foundation of the world. . . ." Thus, before "in the beginning" something other than a static situation existed. A choice was made and that choice shows forth thought and will. We were chosen in him before the creation of the world. The same thing is emphasized in 1 Peter 1:20, where the sacrificial death of Jesus is said to have been "foreordained before the foundation of the world." Likewise Titus 1:2 says that God promised eternal life "before the world began."

This is very striking. How can a promise be made before the world began? To whom could it be made? The Scripture speaks of a promise made by the Father to the Son or to the Holy Spirit because, after all, at this particular point of sequence there was no one else to make the promise to.

Finally, the same point is made in 2 Timothy 1:9, where we read about God, "Who hath saved us, and called us with an holy calling, not according to our works, but according to his own purpose and grace, which was given us in Christ Jesus before the world began."

We are faced, therefore, with a very interesting question: When did history begin? If one is thinking with the modern concept of the space-time continuum, then it is quite obvious that time and history did not exist before "in the beginning." But if we are thinking of history in contrast to an eternal, philosophic other or in contrast to a static eternal, then history began before Genesis 1:1.

We must choose our words carefully here, of course. How shall we talk about the situation before "in the beginning"? To avoid confusion, I have chosen the word *sequence,* in contrast to the word *time* as used in the concept of the space-time continuum. It will remind us that something was there before "in the beginning" and that it was more than a static eternal.

After creation, God worked into time and communicated knowledge to man who was in time. And since he did this, it is quite obvious that it is not the same to God before creation and after creation. The Scripture pictures this before "in the beginning" as something that can be stated. While we cannot exhaust the meaning of what is involved, we can know it truly. It is a reasonable concept, one that we can discuss.

This subject is not merely theoretical. What is involved is the reality of the personal God in all eternity in contrast to the philosophic other or impersonal everything which is frequently the twentieth-century theologian's concept of God. What is involved is the reality of the personal God in contrast to a theoretical unmoved mover, or man's purely subjective thought protection. There is more here than contentless, religious truth achieved through some sort of existential leap. Consequently, when we read, "in the beginning God created the heavens and the earth," we are not left with something hung in a vacuum: Something existed before creation and that something was personal and not static; the Father loved the Son; there was a plan; there was communication; and promises were made prior to the creation of the heavens and the earth.

This whole conception is rooted in the reality of the Trinity. Without the Trinity, Christianity would not have the answers that modern man needs. As I have said elsewhere, Jean Paul Sartre well pointed out the basic philosophic problem that faces us: the fact that something—rather than nothing—is there. This is the incontestable and irreducible minimum for beginning to move as a man. I cannot say nothing is there; it is quite plain that something is there. Furthermore, it is also clear that this something that is there has two parts. I am there and something in contrast to myself is there.

This leads us, of course, to the modern notion of Being. Being is there. But the question immediately arises: "Has it always been there?"[1] This is modern man's basic mystery.

Man is shut up to relatively few answers. I think we often fail to understand that the deeper we go into study at this point, the simpler the alternatives become. In almost any profound question, the number of final possibilities is very few indeed. Here there are four: (1) Once there was absolutely nothing and now there is something, (2) Everything began with an impersonal something, (3) Everything began with a personal something, and (4) There is and always has been a dualism.

The first of these, that once there was absolutely nothing and now there is something, has, as far as I know, never been seriously propounded by anyone, and the reason for this is clear. For this explanation to be true, *nothing* must really be *nothing*—totally nothing—neither mass nor motion nor energy nor personality. Think, for example, of a circle that contains everything there is and there is nothing in the circle, then remove the circle. This is the concept of absolute nothing. As I say, I know no one who has propounded the concept that all that now is has come out of such absolute nothing.

The fourth notion, that of an eternal dualism, can be dealt with rather quickly because it has never stood under close analysis, for men naturally press on behind the dualism and its particulars toward a unity by which to comprehend the duality. This is true whether it is the dualism of 19 electromagnetism and gravity, or some shadowy Tao behind Yin and Yang. Parallel dualisms (for example, ideas or ideals and matter, or brain and mind) either tend to stress one at the expense of the other or leave the unsatisfied question of how they march on together with no reason for doing so.

In contrast to this, the impersonal beginning, the notion that everything began with an impersonal something, is the consensus of the Western world in the twentieth century. It is also the consensus of almost all Eastern thinking. Eventually, if we go back far enough, we come to an impersonal source. It is the view of scientism, or what I have called elsewhere modern modern science, and is embodied in the notion of the uniformity of natural causes in a closed system. And it is also the concept of much modern theology if one presses it back far enough.

An impersonal beginning, however, raises two overwhelming problems which neither the East nor modern man has come anywhere near solving. First, there is no real explanation for the fact that the external world not only exists but has a specific form. Despite its frequent attempt to reduce the concept of the personal to the area of chemical or psychological conditioning, scientific study demonstrates that the universe has an express form. One can go from particulars to a greater unity, from the lesser laws to more and more general laws or super-laws. In other words, as I look at the Being which is the external universe, it is obviously not just a handful of pebbles thrown out there. What is there has form. If we assert the existence of the impersonal as the beginning of the universe, we simply have no explanation for this kind of situation.

Second, and more important, if we begin with an impersonal universe, there is no explanation of personality. In a very real sense the question of questions for all generations—but overwhelmingly so for modern man—is "Who am I?" For when I look at the "I" that is me and then look around to those who face me and are also men, one thing is immediately obvious: Man has a mannishness. You find it wherever you find man—not only in the men who live today, but in the artifacts of history. The assumption of an impersonal beginning can never adequately explain the personal beings we see around us, and when men try to explain man on the basis of an original impersonal, man soon disappears.[2]

In short, an impersonal beginning explains neither the form of the universe nor the personality of man. Hence it gives no basis for understanding human relationships, building just societies or engaging in any kind of cultural effort. It's not just the man in the university who needs to understand these questions. The farmer, the peasant, anyone at all who moves and thinks needs to know. That is, as I look and see that something is there, I need to know what to do with it. The impersonal answer at any level and at any place at any time of history does not explain these two basic factors—the universe and its form, and the mannishness of man. And this is so whether it is expressed in the religious terms of pantheism or modern scientific terms.

But the Judeo-Christian tradition begins with the opposite answer. And it is upon this that our whole Western culture has been built. The universe had a personal beginning—a personal beginning on the high order of the Trinity. That is, before "in the beginning" the personal was already there. Love and thought and communication existed prior to the creation of the heavens and the earth.

Modern man is deeply plagued by the question "Where do love and communication come from?" Many artists who pour themselves out in their paintings, who paint bleak messages on canvas, many singers, many poets and dramatists are expressing the blackness of the fact that   21 while everything hangs upon love and communication, they don't know where these come from and they don't know what they mean.

The biblical answer is quite otherwise: Something was there before creation. God was there; love and communication were there; and therefore, prior even to Genesis 1:1, love and communication are intrinsic to what always has been.

The Trinity

If we press on in a slightly different way, we can see even more of the nature of the God who existed prior to creation. In Genesis 1:26 we read: "And God said, Let us make man in our image. . . ." As we have seen in the New Testament, God the Father not only loved the Son but made a promise to him. And so we should not be taken by surprise when we read the phrase *Let us* or the phrase in Genesis 3:22, "the man is become as one *of us.*" This same phrase also occurs in Isaiah 6:8: "Also I heard the voice of the Lord, saying, Whom shall I send, and who will go *for us?*"[3]

The teaching that the Trinity was already there in the beginning is especially emphasized in John 1:1-3. As a matter of fact, the concept has particular force because it picks up the first phrase of Genesis and makes it, it seems to me, into a technical term: "*In the beginning* already was [the Greek imperfect here is better translated *already was* than *was*] the Word and the Word already was with God and the Word already was God. The same was in the beginning with God." Then in the third verse the Greek aorist tense[4] is used in contrast to the imperfects that preceded it: "All things were made [*became*] by him. . . ." Thus we find first a statement that the Word already was, but then in sharp contrast to this we find something new was brought into being "in the beginning" when he who already was there made what now is.

Furthermore, we know who the personality called the Word (Logos) is; verses 14-15 make it plain: "And the Word was [*became*] flesh, and dwelt among us . . . , [and] John [John the Baptist] bare witness of him. . . ." Of course, the one John bare witness to is Jesus Christ.

Here too there is a contrast between the imperfect and the aorist in the Greek. The one who already was [the imperfect tense] the Word in the beginning and who had a part in creating all things, became [aorist tense] flesh. I believe that John, the writer of the Gospel, deliberately made such a distinction. That is, in the "beginning" this Word already was, but subsequent to this and in contrast to it there were two absolute beginnings: The first occurred when all things were made (became), and the second when the Word became flesh. Thus, the absolute beginning of the creation and the absolute beginning of the incarnation stand in contrast to the *always wasness* of the Logos. In John 1:1 this is related to the term, "in the beginning." I think, therefore, that "in the beginning" is a technical term meaning "in the beginning of all that was created," in contrast to the pre-existence of the non-static personal-infinite, Triune God, who did the creating out of nothing.

The phrase "in the beginning" is repeated in Hebrews 1:10, and, as in John 1:1-3, it emphasizes the fact that Christ was already there before creation and was active in creation. That same idea is repeated, though not the phrase itself, in Colossians 1:16-17, because there we are told that "by him were all things created." Furthermore, 1 Corinthians 8:6 contains an interesting parallel: "But to us there is but one God, the Father, of whom are all things, and for whom we exist; and one Lord Jesus Christ, by whom are all things, and we exist by him." Paul sets forth a parallel between the Father creating and the Son creating.

Thus we have considerable detail concerning the specific relation of the Trinity to the act of creation. It is true, of course, that the part of the Holy Spirit in creation is not as clear as that of the Father and the Son, but it seems to me that Genesis 1:2 does make his presence known: "And the earth was without form, and void; and darkness was upon the face of the deep. And the Spirit of God moved upon the face of the waters." I realize that there is some question about how the phrase "Spirit of God" should be understood here, but certainly the Bible, the Old and New Testaments together, makes a point of saying that the Trinity was there and that the Father and the Son took part in the process of creating.

I would repeat, therefore, that Genesis 1:1 does not depict an absolute beginning with nothing before it. God was there—and then came creation.

The historic Christian position concerning Genesis 1:1 is the only one which can be substantiated, the only one which is fair and adequate to the whole thrust of Scripture. "In the beginning" is a technical term stating the fact that at this particular point of *sequence* there is a creation *ex nihilo*—a creation out of nothing. All that is, except for God himself who already has been, now comes into existence. Before this there was a personal existence—love and communication. Prior to the material universe (whether we think of it as mass or energy), prior to the creation of all else, there is love and communication. This means that love and communication are *intrinsic*. And hence, when modern man screams for love and communication (as he so frequently does), Christians have an answer: There is value to love and value to communication because it is rooted into what intrinsically always has been.

The Root of the Biblical Doxology

There is a phrase in the book of Jeremiah that Christians

should engrave upon their hearts: "The portion of Jacob is not like them [the idols made by men]: for he is the former of all things" (Jer. 10:16). This is the root of the biblical doxology—"unto him"—not it! God is not like those idols made of wood and stone, nor is he like those gods that are merely the extension of men's minds. He is the personal God who was there as the former of all things. He is our portion, and he was before all else.

What a sharp contrast to the new theology! The problem in the new theology is to know whether God is there at all. The new theologians are saying the word *God* but never knowing whether there is anyone back of the word and therefore not being able to pray. As Paul Tillich once said in Santa Barbara, "No, I do not pray, but I meditate." The Christian, however, not only says that God is really there but that he was there, that he always has been there, and that he is "my portion" now.

Revelation 4:11 contains a great doxology to this One. Unfortunately, the King James translation does not give its full force. The first phrase should read: "Worthy art thou, our Lord and our God." This reminds us of Jeremiah's phrase, "He is our portion." He is *our* Lord and *our* God. Then the verse continues: "Worthy art thou, our Lord and our God, to receive the glory and the honor and the power: for thou didst create all things, and because of thy will they were, and were created" (ASV). The New English Bible correctly translates it in modern terms: "By thy will they were created, and have their being!" This is the Christian cosmogony.

Here is an answer for modern man overwhelmed by the problem of being, by knowing that something is there and yet not being able to understand it: Everything which has being, except God himself, rests upon the fact that God willed and brought it into creation. With this I understand why being is there and why it has form, and I understand that particular part of being which I myself am and the mannishness (personality) that I find in me. Things fall into place, not through a leap in the dark, but through that which makes good sense and can be discussed. Once and for all, God did create the being of the external world and man's existence. They are not God and they are not an extension of God, but they exist because of an act of the will of that which is personal and which existed prior to their being.

How contrary this is to today's whole drift both in the theological and in the secular world as it rolls and drifts and speaks of the intrinsically impersonal! And how distinct from any form of intrinsic dualism! Rather, this is the biblical answer to the twentieth-century dilemma.

Often in a discussion someone will say, "Didn't God, then, if he is personal and if he loves, need an object for his love? Didn't he *have to* create? And therefore, isn't the universe just as necessary to him as he is to the universe?" But the answer is, No. He did not have to create something face-to-face with himself in order to love, because there already was the Trinity. God could create by a free act of the will because before creation there was the Father who loved the Son and there was also the Holy Spirit to love and be loved. In other words, God had someone face-to-face with himself in the three persons of the Trinity. Our forefathers were certainly right when they formulated the Nicene and the Chalcedonian Creeds and insisted on the true Trinity in all its force. This wasn't just some passing Greek philosophic concept. When Greek thinking raised these questions, the Christians saw that in what the Bible taught they had the answer. Everything hangs on this point—and at no time more than today.

Thus, we know why being in the modern sense is there rather than nothing being there. No wonder that we read in Revelation: "Worthy art thou, our Lord and our God, to receive the glory and the honor and the power." This Christian doxology is rooted not in an irrational, contentless religious experience that cannot be thought of or discussed, not in the thought-forms that surround us and into which, if we are not careful, we so easily drop, but in a true creation. It is rooted in a meaningful existence where "A" is not "non-A." It is wrong to praise God merely as an upper-story, contentless, religious experience. That is one form of taking his name in vain.

Let us notice too that our praise to God is not first of all in the area of soteriology. If we are being fully scriptural, we do not praise him first because he saved us, but first because he is there and has always been there. And we praise him because he willed all other things, including man, into existence.

Therefore, when we read in Genesis 1:1, "In the beginning God created the heavens and the earth," what a tremendous statement this becomes as we speak into the modern world! Upon this hangs any distinctively Christian answer which is going to be strong enough for men in the twentieth century.

Creation by Fiat

How did God create? We read in Hebrews 11:3, "Through faith we understand that the worlds were framed by the word of God."[5] The phrase I am primarily interested in here is *the word of God.*

First, we have both a parallel with and a distinction from an artist's creation. As a younger Christian, I never thought it right to use the word *creation* for an artist's work. I reserved it for God's initial work alone. But I have come to realize that this was a mistake, because, while there is indeed a difference, there is also a very important parallel. The artist conceives in his thought-world and then he brings forth into the external world. This is true of an   27 artist painting a canvas, a musician composing a piece of music, an engineer designing a bridge or a flower arranger making a flower arrangement. First there is the conception in the thought-world and then a bringing forth into the external world. And it is exactly the same with God. God who existed before had a plan, and he created and caused these things to become objective. Furthermore, just as one can know something very real about the artist from looking at his creation, so we can know something about God by looking at his creation. The Scripture insists that even after the fall we still know something about God on this basis.

And yet the differences between the artist and God are overwhelming, because we, being finite, can only create in the external world out of that which is already there. The artist reaches over and uses his brush and his pigments. The engineer uses steel and pre-stressed concrete for his bridge. Or the flower arranger uses the flowers, the moss and the rocks and the pebbles that were already there. God is quite different. Because he is infinite, he created originally out of nothing—*ex nihilo*. There was no mass, no energy particles, before he created. We work through the manifestation of our fingers. He, in contrast, created merely, as it says in the passage we have just quoted from Hebrews, by his word. Here is power beyond all that we can imagine in the human, finite realm. He was able to create and shape merely by his spoken word.

A few years ago in England some Christians became excited about the Big Bang theory, thinking that it favored Christianity. But they really missed the point—either the point of Scripture or the Big Bang theory or both. The simple fact is that what is given in Genesis 1:1 has no relationship to the Big Bang theory—because from the scriptural viewpoint, the primal creation goes back beyond the basic material or energy. We have a new thing created by God out of nothing by fiat, and this is the distinction.

Suppose you could take back everything in the world and compress it into a heavy molecule only three centimeters in each direction, and suppose that everything came from that. This is still no answer to man's basic problem, because it does not explain how that molecule came to be there or how from that molecule could come the form and complexity of the present universe, or something as personal and as mannish as man. For this the scriptural answer is needed.

And 2 Peter 3:5 is another expression of that answer: "For this they [the scoffers who say that Christ is not really coming again] willingly are ignorant of, that by the word of God the heavens were of old, and the earth standing out of the water and in the water." God by fiat brought the world into existence.

But we should point out something further: "But the heavens and the earth, which are now, by the same word are kept in store, reserved unto fire against the day of judgment and perdition of ungodly men" (2 Pet. 3:7). This passage thus reflects not only creation but the flow of history—both its beginning and its continuation. God not only brought the heavens and the earth into existence by divine fiat, he still works into history in the same way. He has not become a slave of his creation. Nor is he a slave of history because he made history as it is now. History is going somewhere—there is a flow to history. And the same "word of God" will come forth when God speaks again with judgment and with fire. Thus while there is a uniformity of natural causes in the external world that God had made, it is not in a closed system. God can still speak when he will, and Peter says that one day in history he indeed will speak again, with judgment.

This concept of creation by a spoken word is wonderfully expressed in two passages in the Psalms, in which true propositional truth in verbalized form is spoken with total beauty. The first is in Psalm 33:6, 9: "By the word of the LORD were the heavens made. . . ." Notice how this exactly parallels the New Testament passages above—by the word of the Lord. And then notice in the ninth verse: "For he spake, and it was." You should draw a big black line through the word *done* as it appears in the King James translation, for it doesn't appear in the original, and I don't know why the translators ever put it there. It spoils the impact and meaning. Rather: "He spoke, and it was." That which was not, on his spoken fiat, became. This is the beginning of the flow of the space-time continuum, history as we know it.

The second passage is in Psalm 148:5: "Let them praise the name of the LORD: for he commanded, and they were created." This is the Old Testament equivalent of Revelation 4:11, the basis of the doxology: God really is there and he made to be all things that are.

It is either not knowing or denying the createdness of things that is at the root of the blackness of modern man's difficulties. Give up creation as space-time, historic reality, and all that is left is what Simone Weil called uncreatedness. It is not that something does not exist, but that it just stands there, autonomous to itself, without solutions and without answers. Once one removes the createdness of all things, meaning and categories can only be some sort of leap, with or without drugs, into an irrational world. Modern man's blackness, therefore, rests primarily upon his losing the reality of the createdness of all things (all things except the personal God who always has been).

But because I and all Christians know truly, even though not exhaustively, "why" something is there, why the world has form and men have mannishness, I can meet a Simone Weil or a modern man in despair and we can talk. There is a discussible answer as to why things are the way they are, and this is the framework for my thankfulness, as it should be for every Christian. Unless we reach back into the things that we have discussed here, even thankfulness for salvation becomes meaningless, because it is suspended in a vacuum. In truth, as Jeremiah says, "The portion of Jacob is not like them: for he is the former of all things." I now can be thankful both for the knowledge of what is and for my salvation in Jesus Christ. For both are rooted in the fact that the portion of Jacob is not like the gods old or new. He is different: He is the former of all things.

chapter 2

**differentiation
and the
creation
of man**

God the Creator is our portion. He calls us to love and to worship him for his bringing into being all that is. The Bible is not silent concerning why this should be so.

"Created"

The word *created* (Heb. *bārā'*) is used only a limited number of times in Scripture. This is especially true of the specific form used in Genesis 1:1, 21, 27 and 5:1-2. In the unfolding creation this is used at three crucial points. The first of these is the point at which God created out of nothing (Gen. 1:1); the second the point at which God created conscious life (Gen. 1:21); and the third the point at which God created man (Gen. 1:27).

The third passage is especially interesting because the word *created* in this special form is repeatedly used: "So God *created* man in his own image, in the image of God *created* he him; male and female *created* he them." It is as though God put exclamation points here to indicate that there is something special about the creation of man. This is strengthened as we turn to the summary in Genesis 5:1-2: "This is the book of the generations of Adam. In the day that God *created* man, in the likeness of God made he him; Male and female *created* he them; and blessed them, and called their name Adam, in the day when they were *created*." Both passages put a triple emphasis on the word. God is saying that three aspects of creation—creation out of nothing, creation of conscious life, and creation of man—are unique.

Differentiation

Genesis 1:2 reads: "And the earth was without form [this can be translated that the earth was waste], and void; and darkness was upon the face of the deep." At this point in the process of creation that which has been made up to this time lacks differentiation. In other words, it would seem that we have here the creation of *bare being*. What God has made is without form; there is no differentiation between the parts. Then, as we go on into the third verse and beyond, we find a continuing, unfolding differentiation. There are thus two steps: (1) creation out of nothing and (2) differentiation.

The second step is not to be confused with the first. For one thing, in almost every case differentiation is introduced with *let*. For example, "And God said, Let there be light: and there was light" (Gen. 1:3) or, "Let there be a firmament in the midst of the waters: . . . and it was so" (Gen. 1:6-7). In short, God says something like "Let it be this way," a different kind of act than creation itself.

The word *let* has an even more general usage in some verses. For example, in Genesis 1:14, after God says, "Let there be lights in the firmament of the heaven," he goes on to say, "Let them be for signs, and for seasons, and for days, and years." And in the second portion of verse 26 he says, "and let them [men] have dominion." That is, in these places God is not so much making something come into being, or even differentiating it as being, as he is indicating what this sort of being means. Note, however, that in most of the uses of the word *let* in this chapter God is still working by fiat, just as he did in creation. He is saying, "Let this take place," and it takes place.

36

True Communication and Exhaustive Communication
We are considering here matters which lie far in the past and concern cosmic events. That raises a question: Can we really talk in any meaningful sense at all about them? It is helpful, first, to distinguish between true communication and exhaustive communication. What we claim as Christians is that, when all of the facts are taken into consideration, the Bible gives us true knowledge although not exhaustive knowledge. Man as a finite creature is incapable of handling exhaustive knowledge anyway. There is an analogy here with our own communication between men; we communicate to each other truly, but we do not communicate exhaustively. A Christian holding the strongest possible view of inspiration still does not claim exhaustive knowledge at any point.

The Bible is a most efficient book. We must remember its purpose: It is God's message to fallen men. The Old Testament gave men what they needed from the Fall till the first coming of Christ. The Old and New Testaments together give all that men need from the Fall until the second coming of Christ. Many other details which we need are also given, but the main purpose is kept central and uncluttered. For example, angels are touched on many times, but the Bible is not a book on "angelology." What is told us about angels is true and propositional but always in relation to men. Heaven is the same; we are given factual knowledge concerning what we need to know about heaven but not a great deal of detail. Cosmic creation is included because we need to know these things which were before the Fall. What the Bible tells us is propositional, factual and true truth, but what is given is in relation to men. It *is* a scientific textbook in the sense that where it touches the cosmos it is true, propositionally true. When we get to heaven, what we learn further will no more contradict the facts the Bible now gives us than the New

Testament contradicts the Old. The Bible is *not* a scientific textbook if by that one means that its purpose is to give us exhaustive truth or that scientific fact is its central theme and purpose.

Therefore, we must be careful when we say we know the flow of history: We must not claim, on the one hand, that science is unnecessary or meaningless, nor, on the other hand, that the extensions we make from Scripture are absolutely accurate or that these extensions have the same validity as the statements of Scripture itself. But all that does not change the fact that biblical revelation is propositional, to be handled on the basis of reason in relationship to science and coordinated with science. The content of Scripture is not upper-story, and the whole of Scripture is revelational.[1]

As we look at the differentiations that occur when God says "Let it be this way," we can have confidence that this is true history, but that does not mean that the situation is exhaustively revealed or that all our questions are answered. This was the case with our forefathers; it is so for us and will be for everyone who comes after us. Indeed, as we stand before God in time to come, even as we see him face to face, his communication then—certainly being more than what we now have—will still not be totally exhaustive, because we who are finite can never exhaust the infinite. What we know can be true and normative and yet not be a completely detailed map containing all of the knowledge which God himself has.

God Divided

After the initial creation out of nothing, therefore, come the various differentiations. The first differentiation comes in Genesis 1:3-4: "And God said, Let there be light: and there was light. And God saw the light, that it was good: and God divided the light from the darkness." (The word *divided,* or *separated,* is the key, for it is repeated over and over throughout this chapter.) The first differentiation is between darkness and light. When I was younger, I was puzzled by the fact that light is referred to at this particular place, and yet today we know that it fits with what science says at this moment. With the splitting of the atom the discussion shifted; light is closely related to energy, and it is not surprising that out of *bare being* light (in contrast to the sun) is spoken of as the first differentiation.

The second differentiation comes in verse 6: "And God said, Let there be a firmament in the midst of the waters, and let it divide the waters from the waters." Some scholars who have tried to minimize the teaching of the Bible have said that the word *firmament* indicates that the Jews had an idea of a brass or iron covering over the world. But this is not the picture at all. *Firmament* simply means "expanse." It is a rather broad word, as we can see from the fact that the *firmament* is where the moon and the sun and the stars are (v. 14). Perhaps for our generation the word *space* would be the best equivalent. But it is also the place where the birds fly (v. 20). In any case, the idea that it is merely a hard covering and reflects a primitive notion of a three-story universe is in error. Rather what is being referred to is differentiation in the area of being—a differentiation of the openness that is about us.

In verse 9 the differentiation continues and concentrates on earth itself: "And God said, Let the waters under the heavens be gathered together into one place, and let the dry land appear: and it was so." Now we have sea and land. There is a constant refining, as it were, as we come down through these steps.

Verse 11 contains a fourth differentiation: "And God said, Let the earth bring forth grass, vegetation, the plant yielding seed, and the fruit tree yielding fruit after its kind, whose seed is in itself, upon the earth: and it was so." So the earth puts forth vegetation and we have here a differentiation between non-life and life of a vegetable sort.

Differentiation continues in verses 14-16 where God makes lights in the firmament and divides the day from the night on the earth. It is verse 16 which gives the most difficulty: "And God made two great lights; the greater light to rule the day, and the lesser light to rule the night: he made the stars also." However, the primary emphasis is that on the earth the day is divided from the night. The primary thrust is a continued differentiation as existence moves from bare being to light (or energy) and on into a differentiated space, areas of water and earth, the non-living, and the living plants, and day and night on the earth.

Verses 20 and 21 take up one of the most crucial differentiations—that between conscious and unconscious life. Let me point out, again, that it is at this particular place that the word *created* in its special form is used: "And God said, Let the waters bring forth abundantly the moving creature that hath life, and fowl that may fly above the earth in the open firmament of heaven. And God *created* great whales [or great sea creatures], and every living creature that moveth, which the waters brought forth abundantly, after their kind, and every winged fowl after his kind: and God saw that it was good." Thus comes conscious life on two levels—conscious life in the waters and conscious life in the air. In fact, a better translation of the second half of verse 20 is "*Let* fowl fly." The word *let* is not in the Hebrew, but the form of the word *to fly* requires it. In other words, *let* is used throughout this section—in verses 3, 6, 9, 11, 14 and now twice in 20. But at this point of conscious life, the unique note of *create* is stressed, just as it was previously at the unique original creation out of nothing.

In verse 24, we come to the seventh differentiation:

"And God said, Let the earth bring forth the living creatures after their kind, cattle, and creeping things, and beasts of the earth after their kind: and it was so" (ASV). In this division conscious life on the earth is distinguished from conscious life in the water and conscious life in the air. At this point, everything has been produced and differentiated with the exception of one thing, and that is man. And so we come, finally, to the distinction which is so overwhelmingly important to us.

God sets man apart from bare being, vegetable life, and the conscious life of fish, birds and animals. Genesis 1:26 reads: "And God said, Let us make man in our image, after our likeness." Man stands in marked contrast to everything which has been created before. First, as we have already seen, the word *create* is applied to him and that means that God made man in a special way. Furthermore, we know something about this special way: Man was made "in the image of God."

We should see this passage in relation to Genesis 2:7, where additional detail is added: "And the LORD God formed man of the dust of the ground, and breathed into his nostrils the breath of life; and man became a living soul." Lest we make too much of the word *soul*, we should note that this word is also used in relation to other living things with conscious life. So in reality the emphasis here is not on the soul as opposed to the body but on the fact that by a specific and definite act God created man to be a living thing with conscious life. God made man in his image by a specific act of creation. This is strongly emphasized, as we saw before, by the fact that the special word *create* is used three times over, in both Genesis 1:27 and 5:1-2.

Genesis 1 and Genesis 2
Some scholars today see Genesis 1 and Genesis 2 as two separate accounts, almost as if they were watertight com- **41**

partments in which nothing from the one relates to any-thing from the other. But, according to Scripture's own exegesis of these chapters, this is not allowable. Actually, the first and second chapters of Genesis form a unit; nei-ther account stands complete in itself. The two passages are complementary, each containing unique material that is important for an understanding of man.

But there is a stronger case for unity than the simple recognition of interplay and overlapping between the two accounts. Jesus himself ties them together. Hence, in order to set this unity aside, we would have to deny the way Jesus approached the two chapters. In answering the Phari-sees' question concerning divorce, Jesus said, "Have ye not read, that he which made them at the beginning made them male and female. . . ." Jesus is alluding here to Gen-esis 1:27. But he continues: "And [God] said, For this cause shall a man leave father and mother, and shall cleave to his wife: and they twain shall be one flesh." These latter words in Matthew 19:4-5 are a quotation from Genesis 2:24. So Jesus puts the passages from Genesis 1 and Gen-esis 2 together as a unit.

Mark 10:6-8 gives further indication of the unity: "But from the beginning of the creation God made them male and female." This hearkens back to Genesis 1:27. Imme-diately following it Jesus says, "For this cause shall a man leave his father and mother, and cleave to his wife." This derives from Genesis 2:24 and thus again the two are linked as one. Then Jesus goes on: "And they twain shall be one flesh: so then they are no more twain, but one flesh." These passages tied together are the basis of Jesus' moral standard concerning marriage. Jesus reaches back, puts together the creation of man in Genesis 1 with the creation of man in Genesis 2 to show a unity that forms the basis for his view of marriage.

More light is shed on the relationship between Genesis 1

and Genesis 2 by a consideration of a literary structure that occurs throughout the entire book of Genesis: First, less important things are dealt with rapidly, and then the things more important to the central theme of the Bible are returned to and developed more fully. This is so, for example, in the account of Isaac and his two sons Jacob and Esau. Esau's story comes first, but it is Jacob's which is most fully developed. Likewise, Genesis 1 first deals briefly with man in his cosmic setting, and then Genesis 2 turns to man and puts him at the center of the theme of the book. The Bible is, as we have said, the book of fallen men. Its purpose is to tell us, on this side of the Fall, who we are and what God wants us to know. Consequently, after God has dealt with man in his cosmic setting in the first chapter of Genesis, he puts man at the center, beginning midway in chapter 2. While the accounts in Genesis 1 and Genesis 2 have a different emphasis in this way, they are not pitted against each other.

The Historicity of Adam and Eve
Jesus' treatment of Genesis 1 and 2 also brings to the fore the issue of the historicity of Adam and Eve. It is difficult to get away from the fact that Jesus was treating Adam and Eve as truly the first human pair in space and time. If we have any questions concerning this, surely they are resolved as we consider other New Testament passages.

Romans 5:12, for example, contains a strong testimony that Adam and Eve were in fact space-time people: "Wherefore, as by one man sin entered into the world, and death by sin. . . ." Thus, there was a first man, one man. Paul continues in verse 14, "Nevertheless death reigned from Adam to Moses, even over them that had not sinned after the similitude of Adam's transgression. . . ." Adam, it is obvious, is viewed as being just as historic as Moses. If this were not the case, Paul's argument would be meaning-   **43** less. Verse 15 strengthens this: "But not as the offence, so also is the free gift. For if through the offence of the one, the many be dead, much more the grace of God, and the gift by grace, which is by the one man, Jesus Christ, hath abounded unto many." Here, therefore, is a parallel between the historicity of Adam (the first man) and two others—Christ and then ourselves. He is dealing with men in history when he deals with "the many," and so he makes a triple parallelism—the historicity of Adam, the historicity of Christ, and the historicity of me.

The point Paul makes in Romans is strengthened still further in 1 Corinthians 15:21-22: "For since by man came death, by man came also the resurrection of the dead. For as in Adam all die, even so in Christ shall all be made alive." The emphasis is again on the parallel between the historicity of Jesus Christ (whom you must remember Paul had seen on the Damascus road) and the historicity of the man he here called Adam. Verse 45 continues the same thrust: "And so it is written, The first man Adam was made a living soul; the last Adam was made a quickening spirit." The "so it is written" alludes to Genesis 2:7. If one wishes to dispense with the historicity of Adam, certainly he must wonder at such a strong parallelism between Adam and Christ.

Often it is said that this parallelism is only Pauline, but the Gospel of Luke gives us exactly the same thing. Tracing the descent of Jesus backwards, Luke lists a number of characters of history, including such people as David, Jesse, Jacob and Abraham, and ends as follows: "Which was the son of Enos, which was the son of Seth, which was the son of Adam, which was the son of God" (Lk. 3:38). Thus we have another triple parallelism—a parallelism between the objective, historic existence of a whole group of people we know to be historic through the Old Testament and New Testament references, the objective, historic existence of Adam and the objective existence of God himself. If we take away the historicity of Adam, we are left rather breathless! If we tamper with this ordinary way of understanding what is written in the Bible, the structure of Christianity is reduced to only an existential leap.

But let us go further. In 1 Timothy 2:13-14, we read: "For Adam was first formed, then Eve. And Adam was not deceived, but the woman being deceived was in the transgression." Here is something additional: Not only is Adam historic, but Eve in the midst of her rebellion is seen to be historic as well. And 2 Corinthians 11:3 further testifies to it: "But I fear, lest by any means, as the serpent beguiled Eve through his subtilty, so your minds should be corrupted from the simplicity that is in Christ." The parallel here is between Eve and myself. Paul appeals to those of us who are objectively real—who are in history—not to fall into a like situation. And without embarrassment, Paul obviously expects his readers to assume with him the historicity of Eve and the historicity of the details set forth in Genesis.

Notice too how clearly this is the case in 1 Corinthians 11:8-9: "For the man is not of the woman, but the woman of the man. Neither was the man created for the woman; but the woman for the man." Here the fact that Eve was created after Adam is an important part of Paul's argument. One would also have to take into account the way in which Paul quotes the early part of Genesis in 1 Corinthians 6:16 and in Ephesians 5:31. (And finally, in 1 John 3:12, Cain is taken as historic, and in Hebrews 11, Abel, Enoch and Noah are placed as parallel to Abraham and all that followed him in history.)

We have, therefore, a strong testimony to the unity of Genesis 1 and 2 and to the historicity of Adam and Eve. They bear the weight of the authority of Paul and Luke as well as that of Jesus.

The Creation of Eve

In Genesis 2 Adam is created prior to Eve. There is no human being standing before him. He is alone. Adam, being created in a specific, unique fashion in the image of God, differentiated from all that has preceded him, finds that nothing corresponds to him. In the Hebrew one can feel the force of this especially in verse 20: "But for Adam there was not found an help meet for him [that is, a helper opposite to him]." The emphasis here is on a counterpart to Adam, someone parallel to him yet someone different. This counterpart, which we now know so very well in the man-woman relationship in life, simply didn't exist at this time. Something wasn't there.

"And the LORD God said, It is not good that the man should be alone; I will make an help meet for him" (Gen. 2:18). And the biblical statement continues: "And the LORD God caused a deep sleep to fall upon Adam, and he slept: and he took one of his ribs, and closed up the flesh instead thereof; and the rib, which the LORD God had taken from the man, made he a woman, and brought her unto the man. And Adam said, This is now [this can be translated *this one at this time* which gives it the historical emphasis] —This one at this time is bone of my bones, and flesh of my flesh: she shall be called Woman, because she was taken out of Man. Therefore shall a man leave his father and his mother, and shall cleave unto his wife, and they shall be one flesh" (Gen. 2:21-24).

The intriguing thing here is that Jesus, in a passage we have already looked at in the New Testament (Matt. 19:4-5), calls what is given in verse 24 a direct statement of God. God says this because of the way Eve was made, taken out of the man. So it is hard to tamper with this straightforward way of speaking of the early portion of Genesis without losing the possibility of real meaning in language or in communication. We are told that God made woman in this particular way.

Certainly the fact of the woman's creation out of the man has a very definite philosophic importance, because it means that mankind is really a unit. Man didn't just come out of nowhere. Nor has he sprung up from numerous starts. There was a real beginning, a beginning in a real unity in one man, one individual, differentiated from all that preceded him, and then differentiated in terms of male and female. It is this picture of man which gives strength to the Christian concept of the unity of mankind. The world today is trying to find a basis for claiming all men are one, but the Christian does not have this problem, for he understands why mankind is really united.

Furthermore, we can begin to understand something about marriage because God himself ties the marriage bond into the reality of the unity of mankind. Hence, we can understand something of that particular union when the male and female constitute one whole, become one flesh. Man, with a capital M, equals male and female, and the one-man, one-woman union reunites that unity.

As Christians we should not let this section of Genesis in regard to the creation of Eve be shoved aside as something unimportant. At first it might seem that we would not lose much, yet eventually it would bring real destruction. The Bible describes the creation of Eve as a specific differentiation, in its own way as much a differentiation as the creation of Adam himself.

There is special force, therefore, in Genesis 5:1-2: "This is the book of the generations of mankind. In the day that God created man, in the likeness of God made he him; Male and female created he them; and blessed them, and called their name mankind [or *man*], in the day when they were created."[2] The second time the word *created* is used in this passage, it appears in relationship to both male and female. This is parallel to Genesis 1:27: "Male and female *created* he them." The structure is now complete.

Hence, to summarize where we are in the flow of history, we can say that there is first creation out of nothing, then differentiation in various forms, then differentiation of man from all that preceded, and then, in a very special way, differentiation of Eve from Adam, woman from man. The whole sequence testifies to Adam and Eve standing in space-time history.

The Image of God

What is it that differentiates Adam and Eve from the rest of creation? We find the answer in Genesis 1:26: "And God said, Let us make man in our image. . . ." What differentiates Adam and Eve from the rest of creation is that they were created in the *image of God.* For twentieth-century man this phrase, *the image of God,* is as important as anything in Scripture, because men today can no longer answer that crucial question, "Who am I?" In his own naturalistic theories, with the uniformity of cause and effect in a closed system, with an evolutionary concept of a mechanical, chance parade from the atom to man, man has lost his unique identity. As he looks out upon the world, as he faces the machine, he cannot tell himself from what he faces. He cannot distinguish himself from other things.

Quite in contrast, a Christian does not have this problem. He knows who he is. If anything is a gift of God, this is it—knowing who you are. As a Christian, I know my differentiation. I can look at the most complicated machine that men have made so far or ever will make and realize that, though the machine may do some things that I cannot do, I am different from it. If I see a machine that is stronger than I am, it doesn't matter. If it can lift a house, I am not disturbed. If it can run faster than I can, its speed doesn't threaten me. If I am faced with a giant computer which can never be beaten when it plays checkers—even when I realize that never in history will I or any man be able to beat it—I am not crushed. Others may be overwhelmed intellectually and psychologically by the fact that a man can make a machine that can beat him at his own games, but not the Christian.

The Christian knows that in the flow of history man comes from a different origin. It is not that God has not made both man and the great machine of the universe, but that he has made man different from the rest of the universe. And that which differentiates man from the machine is that his basic relationship is upward rather than downward or horizontal. He is created to relate to God in a way that none of the other created beings are.

It is on the basis of being made in the image of God that everything is open to man. Suddenly, personality does not slip through my fingers. I understand the possibility of fellowship and of personality. I understand that because I am made in the image of God and because God is personal, both a personal relationship with God and the concept of fellowship as fellowship has validity. The primary factor is that my relationship is upward. Of course, I have relationships downward as well, but I am differentiated from all that is below me and I am no longer confused.

This differentiation makes genuine love possible. One cannot picture machines as loving. Though one computer may combine with another computer to bring forth a combined answer to some sort of question, we would not call this a love relationship. Furthermore, if we are made in the image of God, we are not confused as to the possibility of communication; and we are not confused concerning the possibility of revelation, for God can reveal propositional truth to me as I am made in his image. Finally (as theologians have long pointed out), if man is made in the image of God, the Incarnation, though it has many mysteries, is **49** not foolishness. The Incarnation is not irrational as it surely is if man sees himself as only the finite in face-to-face relationship with a philosophic other.

Consequently, I should be thankful for the comprehension given here in Genesis—that in the flow of history man has been made in the image of God, for it gives an intellectual, emotional and psychological basis to my understanding of who I am.

The Dominion of Man

It is on the basis of being created in the image of God that man has dominion over the other things in the world about him. It isn't that man is simply stronger; as a matter of fact, he isn't always stronger. Dominion itself is an aspect of the image of God in the sense that man, being created in the image of God, stands between God and all which God chose to put under man. As that which was created, man is no higher than all that has been created, but as created in the image of God he has the responsibility to consciously care for all that which God put in his care.

Furthermore, being created in the image of God frees us from the burden of thinking that whatever *is* therefore must be *right*. We have been given a dominion which puts a moral responsibility on us. We don't need to succumb therefore to the ethics of the Marquis de Sade, where might or whatever is, is right.

But let us go further. We read in Genesis 1:26: ". . . and let them have dominion over the fish of the sea, and over the fowl of the air, and over the cattle, and over all the earth, and over every creeping thing that creepeth upon the earth." These words are soon repeated: "And God blessed them, and God said unto them, Be fruitful, and multiply, and fill [the King James' *replenish* is inaccurate] the earth, and subdue it; and have dominion over the fish of the sea, and over the fowl of the air, and over every living thing that moveth upon the earth. And God said, Behold I have given you every herb bearing seed, which is upon the face of the earth, and every tree, in which is the fruit of a tree yielding seed; to you it shall be for meat" (Gen. 1:28-29). We should clarify this translation, for the word *herb* is not meant to be a contrast with other plants, but rather indicates the total plant life, and the phrase *bearing seed* is, in the Hebrew, "seeding seeds." Furthermore, the word *meat* simply means "food," not meat as opposed to vegetables. So perhaps one could more clearly translate verse 29 this way: "I have given you every plant seeding seeds, which is upon the face of the earth, and every tree which is the fruit of a tree seeding seeds; to you it shall be for food." Thus, man in his dominion is to have the plants for his use.

A further implication of his dominion is brought out in Genesis 2:19-20: "And out of the ground the LORD God formed every beast of the field, and every fowl of the air; and brought them unto Adam to see what he would call them: and whatsoever Adam called every living creature, that was the name thereof. And Adam gave names to all cattle and to the fowl of the air, and to every beast of the field." Thus the implications of his dominion extended beyond the plant kingdom all the way to that which has conscious life.

Perhaps one of the most striking expressions of the concept of man's dominion is found in Psalm 8:5-8:

For thou hast made him a little lower than the angels, and hast crowned him with glory and honor. Thou hast made him to have dominion over the works of thy hands; thou hast put all things under his feet: All sheep and all oxen, yea, and beasts of the field; The fowl of the air, and the fish of the sea, and whatsoever passeth through the paths of the sea.

This passage does, of course, have a prophetic reference to **51**

Jesus Christ, but it is also applicable to mankind in general. All of these elements of reality—animals, birds and marine life—are under the dominion of man, and man has a responsibility for them as well as the right to properly use them.

Psalm 115:16 further testifies to the fact but adds a qualification: "The heaven, even the heavens, are the LORD's: but the earth hath he given the children of men." Not all of creation, therefore, but a certain area is spoken of as being specifically put under man's reign.

By the way, this does not mean that man as he was originally created had no work to do: "And the LORD God took the man, and put him into the Garden of Eden to dress it and to keep it" (Gen. 2:15). As we shall see later, the work he was then to perform was not work as we now know it, but man's life was not just one long period of indolence. Man had work to do before the Fall. He was given dominion, and even though he administers it very badly since the Fall, he still has that dominion.

The Image of God and Fallen Man

It is important to note that fallen man still retains something of the image of God. The Fall separates man from God, but it does not remove his original differentiation from other things. Fallen man is not less than man. Thus we read in Genesis 9:6: "Whoso sheddeth man's blood, by man shall his blood be shed: for in the image of God made he man." Man is such a special creation that to take his life in a wanton, murderous way deserves a particular punishment. I sometimes feel that often the hue and cry against capital punishment today does not so much rest upon humanitarian interest or even an interest in justice, but rather in a failure to understand that man is unique. The simple fact is that Genesis 9:6 is a sociological statement: The reason that the punishment for murder can be so severe is that man, being created in the image of God, has a particular value—not just a theoretical value at some time before the Fall, but such a value yet today.

We find a parallel in James 3:9: "Therewith [speaking of our tongues] bless we the Lord and Father; and therewith curse we men, who are made after the likeness of God" (ASV). This likeness is parallel to the term, *the image of God*.

The Christian, therefore, has a sociological base which is extremely strong. As humanists are fighting today against prejudice, they have little philosophical base for their battle. But as a Christian I do: No matter who I look at, no matter where he is, every man is created in the image of God as much as I am.

So the Bible tells me who I am. It tells me how I am differentiated from all other things. I do not need to be confused, therefore, between myself and animal life or between myself and the complicated machines of the second half of the twentieth century.

Suddenly I have value, and I understand how it is that I am different. I understand how it is that God can have fellowship with me and give me revelation of a propositional nature. Furthermore, I can see that all men are so differentiated from non-man, and I must look upon them as having great value. Coming back to Genesis 9:6: Anyone who murders a man is not just killing one who happens to be of a common species with me, but one of overwhelming value, one made in the image of God. As James says, any man, no matter who he is, stranger or friend, a Christian or someone who is still in rebellion against God, is made after the likeness of God. A man is of great value not for some less basic reason but because of his origin.

Thus the flow of history has tremendous implications for every aspect of our lives. I stand in the flow of history. I know *my* origin. My lineage is longer than the Queen of

England's. It does not start at the Battle of Hastings. It does not start with the beginnings of good families, wherever or whenever they lived. As I look at myself in the flow of space-time reality, I see my origin in Adam and in God's creating man in his own image.

chapter 3

God
and his
universe

As the Creator, God shapes and fashions and brings bare
being into form—a form which is truly reflective of the
One who fashions it. And when God is finished with this
process what he has made speaks of the God who made it.

The Goodness of Creation

Genesis 1 tells us over and over again an important thing
about this creation: In verse 4 we read, "And God saw the
light, that it was good." The phrase *that it was good* is
repeated in verses 10, 12, 18, 21 and 25. And verse 31
sums up the whole of God's judgment: "And God saw
everything that he had made, and, behold, it was very
good." This is not a relative judgment, but a judgment of
the holy God who has a character and whose character is
the law of the universe. His conclusion: Every step and
every sphere of creation, and the whole thing put together
—man himself and his total environment, the heavens and
the earth—conforms to myself.

Everything at each of the various levels of creation fulfills the purpose of its creation. The machine part of the
universe acts with perfect machineness. The animals and
the plants act with their animalness and their plantness in
perfection. Man stands at his particular level of creation as
being in the image of God and having a reference upward
rather than downward, and God is able to say that man,   **57**

too, in his mannishness at this particular point in space-time history, is equally good: "Man conforms to myself on his level of creation."

Thus we find a doxology of all creation—everything glorifying God on its own level. The machine as machine praising and glorifying God, the man as a man, and everything in between, doing likewise. Even though many of these beings are not at all conscious of what they are doing, they are speaking for God in all his wonder and glorifying him in fulfilling the purpose for which they were made. There is no sin. Each thing stands in a proper relationship to God and speaks of what God is. And because each thing is functioning in the total context of what God is (God's being there as the Creator) and because each is functioning perfectly on the level for which it was made, all things are fulfilled on their own level—the machine, the animal, and man himself.

Tillich would tell us that man equals fallen man. But in Genesis the mannishness of man is to be found not in his fallenness, but in the circle in which he was created; it is to be found in his being in the image of God and in relationship to the God who is there. The infinite, triune God himself can look over all that he has created and say, "This is perfect, man is good—body and soul, male and female. The entire man is good. The unity of the individual man is good." Thus we find here a complete rejection of the common notion that the Fall was sexual in nature, that taking the fruit was actually a reference to the first sexual act. God looks upon man and woman together and says, "All of this is good," and in Genesis 1:28 he tells them to have children.

As we come to the end of the account of creation, we stand in the place of wonder. Creation is past. And yet that does not mean that God ceases to be able to work into the world that he has made. God is not a prisoner of his own universe. By divine fiat God can change the universe that he has created just as by divine fiat he brought it into existence in the first place. There was, for example, a fiat changing the universe after the Fall of man. And that God can work by fiat into the universe he has made is an important thing for twentieth-century men to comprehend. We will take it up in detail later.

Day
Before we move on there is a point we need to consider. This is the concept of *day* as related to creation. What does *day* mean in the days of creation? The answer must be held with some openness. In Genesis 5:2 we read: "Male and female created he them; and blessed them, and called their name Adam, in the *day* when they were created." As it is clear that Adam and Eve were not created simultaneously, day in Genesis 5:2 does not mean a period of twenty-four hours. In other places in the Old Testament the Hebrew word *day* refers to an era, just as it often does in English. See, for example, Isaiah 2:11, 12 and 17 for such a usage. The simple fact is that *day* in Hebrew (just as in English) is used in three separate senses: to mean (1) twenty-four hours, (2) the period of light during the twenty-four hours, and (3) an indeterminate period of time. Therefore, we must leave open the exact length of time indicated by *day* in Genesis. From the study of the word in Hebrew, it is not clear which way it is to be taken; it could be either way. In the light of the word as used in the Bible and the lack of finality of science concerning the problem of dating, in a sense there is no debate because there are no clearly defined terms upon which to debate.

Creation and the Existence and Character of God
In contrast to all Eastern and most modern theological thinking, Genesis makes plain that the world as we have it   **59**

is not an extension of the essence of God. The fact of creation prevents this conception. And the whole of the Judeo-Christian tradition rooted in this portion of the Bible and the whole of the Bible itself constantly bears testimony to that idea. The world is not just a dream of God but is really there, separated from God and possessed with an objective reality. But it does speak of what God is. In fact, it speaks loudly and clearly of what God is in four different areas.

First, the external world, even as it stands now since the Fall, speaks of existence itself. As I have pointed out before in reference to Jean Paul Sartre, the basic philosophic problem is that something is there rather than nothing being there. Being exists. Therefore, the first thing that the external, objective world speaks of is the existence of God as truly being. That is, the universe is there, existence is there, God is there.

Second, the universe has order. It is not a chaos. One is able to proceed from the particulars of being to some understanding of its unity. One is able to move ever deeper into the universe and yet never come upon a precipice of incoherence. We find this emphasized in Genesis 1 which points out that God made all these things to produce after their own kind. Here is order. And so it is with the God of Scripture. He is not the philosophic other, nor the impersonal everything, nor that which is chaotic or random. He is a God who is (and I use this word carefully and worshipfully) a *reasonable* God.

Third, the universe speaks of God's character. God not only is and is a God of order and of reason, but God is good. He created a universe that is totally good, and, as it originally came from God by fiat, this too speaks of him.

Fourth, the universe speaks of God as a person. When God made man in his own image, he stated something more fully about himself than he has in any other part of the whole scope of the universe. Angels would also speak of this, but the Bible's emphasis is on man, and it is man that we all know. In the midst of that which is, there is something personal—man. And this gives evidence of the personality of the great Creator of the whole. If God had stopped his creation with the machine or the plant or the animal, there would have been no such testimony. But by making man in his own image, the triune God who communicates and who loves prior to the creation of all else has created something that reflects his personality, his communication and his love. Man can be communicated to by God, because, unlike non-man, man has been made in the image of God. Man is a verbalizing being, and God can communicate to man in verbalization. Man thinks in propositions, and God can communicate to man propositionally in verbalized form.

For example, in Genesis 2:16 we read, "And the LORD God commanded the man, saying, Of every tree of the garden thou mayest freely eat: But of the tree of the knowledge of good and evil, thou shalt not eat of it: for in the day that thou eatest thereof thou shalt surely die." Here we learn that God was in communication with man prior to the time of man's fall. God was in fellowship, a relationship of love, with man. Notice that this communication is not just a first-order, contentless, existential experience but rather true, propositional communication.

Immediately following Adam and Eve's decision to eat the fruit, there is a further indication of God's propositional communication: "And they heard the voice of the LORD God walking in the garden in the cool of the day: and Adam and his wife hid themselves from the presence of the LORD God amongst the trees of the garden. And the LORD God called to Adam and said unto him, Where art thou?" (Gen. 3:8-9). Then, after Adam and Eve answered God's questions, God spoke to them in a series of great propositional statements. Man stood in communication with God both before and after the Fall.

It is likewise true that men communicate among themselves. Each time one man communicates with another, whether he knows it or not, even if he is the greatest blasphemer that ever lived or the atheist swearing at God, even when he swears, even when he says, "There is no God"—he bears testimony to what God is. God has left himself a witness that cannot be removed.

The universe, therefore, speaks of Being existing. It speaks of order and reason. It speaks of a good and reasonable God, and it speaks of a personal God.

The end of man is to stand as a finite, personal being in personal relationship with the infinite, personal God who is there. When we hear the first command of Christ to love God with all our heart and soul and mind, we are not faced with just an abstract duty—a devotional exercise separated from all that is reasonable. Rather we have an infinite reference point that gives meaning to all of our finite reference points. This infinite reference point not only exists, but is personal and can communicate with us and we with him, an infinite reference point whom we may love.

This is the purpose of man: to love God on a personal not a machine level. Other things in the universe are properly on a machine level: the hydrogen atom is a machine. The star system is a machine. Their relationship to God is mechanical. But any time we come to a service and sing the doxology mechanically, we have made a mistake: We are not praising God on the level of who we are.

Of course, man is called upon not just to love God but also to love other men. And suddenly, in this setting, this kind of love becomes a sensible statement. Even the unbelieving man or the blasphemer who falls in love testifies, whether he knows it or not, to the fact of what God is. As bare being exhibits the existence of God, as an originally good universe exhibits the moral goodness of God, so the communication of man to man, and one man's loving another (whether in a man-woman sexual relationship or in the relationship of friendship), testify to what is.

God can say, "Do you want to know something of what I am like? Look at creation as I made it." The universe is not an extension of the essence of God, but in all its parts it does speak of him.

The man-woman relationship is no longer a mockery, or a curse, as it often is for modern man. We know that God did not make man as an individual to stand alone for very long, only being able to love God. For while loving God was the purpose of his creation, God quickly gave him a counterpart—like himself, yet different—that immediately opened up love and communication on man's own level. Therefore, each time we see a truly loving man-woman relationship or a truly loving friend relationship, while these things have great value in themselves, yet we see something more than just mannishness loving mannishness. Each of these at the same time stands as a testimony of who God is.

This is a testimony even after the Fall, as we read in Romans 1:19-20: "Because that which may be known of God is manifest in them; for God hath shewed it unto them. For the invisible things of him from the creation of the world are clearly seen, being understood by things that are made, even his eternal power and Godhead." The point here is that "from the creation" (since the moment of creation) the things that God has made are a testimony to his being, to his goodness and to his personality.

Creation at Peace with Itself
When God made creation, creation was at peace with itself. Genesis 1:29-30 might indicate that the food of both men and beasts included only vegetable life. This is not ex-   **63**

plicitly stated here but it might be implied. A change in man's relationship to the rest of creation may be indicated when God spoke to Noah, instituting another set of covenants and bringing about a change in the flow of history: "Every moving thing that liveth shall be food for you; even as the green herb have I given you all things" (Gen. 9:3). God may be saying something like this: "Previously I gave you all the green plants for food, but now every living thing is yours to eat as well." God does say, "And the fear of you and the dread of you shall be upon every beast of the earth, and upon every fowl of the air, upon all that moveth upon the earth, and upon all the fishes of the sea; into your hand they are delivered" (Gen. 9:2). The full implications are not clear, but considering the restoration of creation, it is clear that at creation, creation was at peace with itself. This does not necessarily mean that trees or even fish or animals *might not* have died of old age, but rather that there would have been no fear of non-being (such as man has) and no fear of violence.

For completeness, we must consider the possibility that perhaps Satan's rebellion had already brought fear and violence into the world prior to man's revolt. This cannot be related to anything the Bible explicitly says, but neither is it excluded as a possibility. This, of course, was C. S. Lewis's view. John 12:31; 14:30 and 16:11 do speak of Satan as the prince of this world. Perhaps he was the prince of this world prior to man's revolt or even prior to man's creation, and not just after man's fall. In Isaiah 14:12-17 (which I do think refers to the fall of Satan) verses 16 and 17 would fit into this concept. In other words it would have been Satan in his primal revolt who brought fear and violence into the world of non-man and thus introduced abnormality. Two facts we do have: (1) This would have occurred after the original creation out of nothing and (2) Satan did revolt before the revolt of man.

History Is Going Someplace

History is not just static as some existentialists or Eastern thinkers would tell us. History is really going someplace. Just as there is a beginning (from a creation *ex nihilo*), history flows and goes on into the future. Scripture also indicates that a time will come when creation is returned to peace with itself. Romans 8:21-23 says, ". . . the creation itself also shall be delivered from the bondage of corruption into the glorious liberty of the glory of the children of God. For we know that the whole creation groaneth and travaileth in pain together until now. And not only they, but ourselves also, who have the first fruits of the Spirit, even we ourselves groan within ourselves, waiting for our adoption, the redemption of our body" (ASV). Verse 20 has already indicated that the creation was not always this way. And there is coming a day when the creation will be restored. It is the same time when the bodies of the Christians will be resurrected.

The phrase in verse 23 indicating that we are yet today waiting for the adoption is interesting. In one sense, a Christian is already adopted (this is considered in the first part of Romans 8), for the Christian having accepted Christ as his Savior has already had his guilt removed, has been justified and is now the child of God. Nevertheless, we wait for an adoption that does not come until the second coming of Christ and the resurrection of our bodies. This full adoption which involves the change in the external world of ourselves (the redemption of our bodies) is associated in verse 23 with the redemption of the whole of creation. Notice too that everyone and everything is in this: "The whole creation groaneth and travaileth in pain *together*." We are all caught. Things are not what they were, but they will be at the time when Christ comes back and our bodies are raised.

We have, I believe, a description of this period in Isaiah

11:6-9: "The wolf also shall dwell with the lamb, and the leopard shall lie down with the kid; and the calf and the young lion and the fatling together; and a little child shall lead them. And the cow and the bear shall feed; their young ones shall lie down together: and the lion shall eat straw like the ox. And the sucking child shall play on the hole of the asp, and the weaned child shall put his hand on the adder's den." This passage does not speak of a psychological change in man's view of nature, but an objective change in the external world.

There is, of course, some difference among Christians as to just what period of time this refers to. There are two possibilities. One is that there is a millenium in which Christ reigns on earth for a thousand years before eternity. This is the opinion that I hold. Some Christians think that these passages refer to eternity. Nonetheless, whether they refer to eternity or to a millenial reign of Christ, it makes no difference to our point here: The creation which God made was at peace with itself and will eventually be restored to peace with itself. In other words, there will come a time when all creation once more speaks, not only of the existence of God and his personality, but also of the goodness of God as the original creation exhibited that goodness.

There is, therefore, in Judeo-Christian thinking in contrast to modern thinking a flow of history—an absolute beginning and an end of the present era of history.

Just as the world was "subjected to vanity" when man fell, so when man is fully restored in the future on the basis of the work of Jesus Christ, the Lamb of God, creation will be restored on the same basis. Every restoration rests upon the finished work of Christ. This includes (1) the restoration that opens the way for the sinner to come back to God, be justified, be counted a child of God, be given purpose in the present life and put into communication with God now, (2) the future restoration in which the Christian's body will be changed at the second coming of Christ and (3) the restoration of all things to the character of the original creation.

Therefore, we read in Revelation 4:11: "Worthy art thou, our Lord and our God, to receive the glory and the honor and the power: for thou didst create all things, and because of thy will they were [existed], and were created" (ASV). So, as we have pointed out, we first praise God because he is the Creator of all things. But surely there is something wrong with the world we are confronted with now. Whether we look at ordinary modern man or the tortured works of modern artists or the world around us, there seems to be a flaw. And indeed the flaw is in man, but it is also in the world around us which is not at peace with itself. The testimony of creation as to the existence and personality of God still stands in the objective universe and in man as man. But as we look out over things and see the sin of man and the creation itself at war with itself, we are left with a problem. As the world now is, its testimony to the goodness of God is not clear. The fifth chapter of Revelation points out what is needed and stands in unity with the statement concerning the original creation in Revelation 4:11. Redemption is the key. It is the Lamb of God who is able, when nothing else in heaven above or earth beneath or under the earth—in other words nothing in creation itself—is able to bring the needed change. The solution was Christ's redemptive work in history, in space and in time, as the Lamb of God.

We are therefore told in Revelation 5:9-11 that man sings to the Lamb of God because man is redeemed: "Thou art worthy to take the book, and to open the seals thereof: for thou wast slain, and hast redeemed to God by thy blood men out of every kindred, and tongue, and people, and nation." The same structure is evident in verses

12-14: "Worthy is the Lamb that was slain [notice this is the past tense because it is past history] to receive the power, and the riches, and the wisdom, and the strength, and the honour, and the glory, and the blessing." Following this verse comes something that is surely related to what we have seen in Romans 8 as to what will happen in the future: "And every created thing which is in the heaven, and on the earth, and under the earth, and on the sea, and all things that are in them, heard I saying unto him that sitteth on the throne, and unto the Lamb, be the blessing, and the honor, and the glory, and the dominion, forever and ever. And the four living creatures said, Amen. And the elders fell down and worshipped" (Rev. 5:13-14—ASV). They worship. They adore. Because at that time in the future all will have come to rest and will be in its place on the basis of Christ's redemptive work as he died on the cross.

Other portions of Scripture implicitly (not explicitly) support this. The ark, for example, not only carried Noah but also the animals. The covenant with Noah in Genesis 9:12-13 and 16 includes not only men, but also every living creature and "the earth." The blood of the Passover in Israel covered not only the firstborn of the Jews but the firstborn of their beasts.

There is to be one great paean of praise to redemption—a redemption that will include not just man but the whole of creation, a time when creation will again speak of the great facts of which it spoke originally. Its existence shows the existence of the God who is. The mannishness of man says God is personal. And all creation will say, "God is good."

chapter 4

**the
point of
decision**

Let us go back to the beginning. Creation is finished. Each created thing is operating in the circle of its own creation, standing in its proper place, and all things are at rest and in balance. Man, as made in the image of God, has a unique place because he has been made different from the machines, the plants and the animals.

To Love God
Jesus once stated exactly that peculiar place man has in the various circles of creation. One of the Pharisees had asked him, "Master, which is the great commandment in the Law?" And Jesus replied, "Thou shalt love the Lord thy God with all thy heart, and with all thy soul, and with all thy mind. This is the first and great commandment" (Mt. 22:36-38). Some fifteen hundred years before this, in Deuteronomy 6:4-6, we find this same concept: "Hear, O Israel: The LORD our God is one LORD: and thou shalt love the LORD thy God with all thine heart, and with all thy soul, and with all thy might. And these words, which I command thee this day, shall be in thine heart." Thus at the time of Moses the central issue is not merely an outward keeping of the commandments but something far more profound. Man is to *love* God in his heart.

But it is equally important—and this is brought out in both Matthew and Deuteronomy—for man to remember   **71** *whom* he is to love. Loving a superior is different from loving an equal. Take, for example, the love of a child for a parent. If a child constantly says, "I love you," and yet at the same time is constantly and openly disobedient, the parent can say, "Your actions do not indicate your love." The reason for this is that there is a hierarchy inherent in the relationship between the parent and child. The two people do not stand on a horizontal plane in every regard. Parenthood involves an "office." As Israel is brought face to face with the loving Creator who is there, Israel is not merely to say, "I love you," rooting their reaction only in emotions. The kind of love proper here is also rooted into obedience simply because of the nature of the relationship between the two parties. Love of the creature toward the Creator must include obedience or it is meaningless. Jesus' teaching in Matthew is the same.

With this principle in mind, then, we can begin to understand Adam and Eve's relationship to God in the early chapters of Genesis. Genesis 2:16-17 reads: "And the LORD God commanded the man, saying, Of every tree of the garden thou mayest freely eat: But of the tree of the knowledge of good and evil, thou shalt not eat of it: for in the day that thou eatest thereof thou shalt surely die." Basically, this command is no different from the commandments in Deuteronomy 6:4-6 and Matthew 22:36-38: The first law for man is to love God with all his heart and all his soul and all his mind. If one is a creature in the presence of the Creator, to love includes to obey.

But something else is involved, for here is the idea that obedience to this law is the purpose of man, the only way that man can be fully man.

Today people constantly ask, "Does man have a purpose?" In some areas of the world man is told that he has meaning only in reference to the state. In other places he is told that he has meaning only in his sexual life. Elsewhere he is told he has meaning only through affluence. But all of these turn to sawdust in his hands. The Bible gives us a quite different answer: The purpose of man—the meaning of man—is to stand in love as a creature before the Creator.

But the man who stands before God stands there in God's image as a true personality, and the love which he is to give is not mechanical. The machine can obey God mechanically; when it does, it is doing all that God meant it to do. The far-flung system of the universe operates, much of it, as a great machine; and as such it fulfills its purpose. That is all it was meant to do. But man is a different being, made in a different circle of creation. He is to love God, not mechanically, but by the wonder of choice. Here stands an unprogrammed part of creation—unprogrammed chemically or psychologically—real man in a real history, a wonder in the midst of a world of uniformity of cause and effect. In the flow of history, man is brought face to face with that for which he has been made—face to face in a loving relationship to the God who is there.

One Tree

Love and obedience in Genesis 3 are placed in the context of a commandment concerning a tree—the tree of the knowledge of good and evil. It is important to note that the test Adam faces does not involve a choice between an evil tree that God has made and a good tree that God has made. For God has made no evil things. If he had, or if God had programmed man so that man must disobey him, then we would have here a concept like the Hindu idea that eventually both good and evil, cruelty and non-cruelty, spring from God and thus are finally equal.

But God has not made a bad tree. He has simply made a tree. And there is nothing intrinsic about this tree that is different in any way from the other trees. Rather, God has simply confronted man with a choice. He could just as well have said, "Don't cross this stream; don't climb this mountain." He is saying, "Believe me and stand in your place as a creature, not as one who is autonomous. Believe me and love me as a creature to his Creator, and all will be well. This is the place for which I have made you."

It is perfectly true that in making man as he did God made the possibility of evil. But the bare possibility of evil is not the actualizing of it. And in making that possibility, God validated choice and validated man as man—a being significant in history. If he had left him without choice, you could speak forever of man being man, man being significant, but it would be only meaningless words.

All love—man to woman and woman to man, or friend to friend—is bound up with choice. Without choice the word *love* is meaningless. And, incidentally, as modern man has lost the concept of choice in the midst of determinism, the word *love* has increasingly become meaningless.

God has indeed made the possibility of man's choosing, including the possibility of choosing wrongly. But God has not made evil. There is not an evil tree and a good tree. There is simply choice. When God finished creating there was nothing made which was contrary to his character.

Let us look more closely at the specific kind of tree. It is not simply the tree of *knowledge* but of a specific kind of knowledge—the knowledge of good and evil. It was not an evil thing to have knowledge. Such a concept would contradict the giving of dominion to man, and be in conflict with Genesis 2:19-20, where man as man had knowledge to give proper names to the creatures.

Adam and Eve already knew good, everything around them was good, and their relationship to God and to each other was good. And in knowledge from God they knew the possibility of evil and its result: "Thou shalt not eat of it: for in the day thou eatest thereof thou shalt surely die"

(Gen. 2:17). What was involved was the experiential knowledge of evil in contrast to God's telling them about evil. They are, of course, finite in contrast to God being infinite. God can know all possible possibilities—even what could be but will not be, as well as all that will be. The Bible makes plain that God, as infinite, knows all possibilities even if they never will be actualized. In 1 Samuel 23:9-29 we are told that God knew (and told David) what would happen in case a certain circumstance occurred, even though the situation changed and thus the circumstance never did occur and the possible result never was actualized.

In the case of Adam and Eve, as finite, they had received from God true knowledge concerning the result of eating and revolt, but when they did revolt they then had experiential knowledge of evil and all the flow of resulting cruelty and sorrow. It was not knowledge as knowledge that was wrong, but *the choice* made against God's loving warning and command.

Notice too that God's command to them was not an unmotivated command, not a bare, unexplained command. Adam and Eve were warned about the result, a loss that involved their own best interests. The command was a rational, propositional command and a loving warning.

So let us look again at Genesis 2:17: "But of the tree of knowledge of good and evil, thou shalt not eat of it: for in the day that thou eatest thereof thou shalt surely die." The last phrase is extremely strong in the Hebrew and could very well be rendered, "dying, thou shalt die." Reformed theology treats this commandment as a covenant of works. That is, first, there are two parties. In one way they are equal (both of them have personalities, the one being in the image of the other), and in another way they are not (one is infinite and the other finite; one is Creator, the other the created). And, second, there is a condition in **75** the midst of the covenant, a condition of love couched in the terms of obedience insofar as it involves a creature before the Creator. Third, there is a promise involved—life. Surely, what is promised here is not just a continuing physical life but rather all of those things which we later know to be life indeed in Jesus Christ our Lord. Of course, man does not need a Savior at this point, because he has not sinned. Thus there is no place here for soteriology, no place for the Lamb of God—not yet. Soteriology is related to fallen man. The promise of life is "fullness of life," just as the penalty is "fullness of death."

Note that in the day, the twenty-four hours, when Adam sinned, he did not physically die. He died in a way that the New Testament labels a "present death." Before a man now accepts Christ as his Savior, it is not just that he will die but that he is already dead. He is separated from God, he has no purpose and no final meaning.

Therefore, in the day that Adam ate, he died. There are three steps in this death. First comes separation from God, the infinite, personal reference point and immediately thereafter meaninglessness in the present life. Even though man continues to breathe, and with his wife brings forth children, he is dead. And to this extent our voices as Christians are joined with the voices from the opposite end of the spectrum—the existentialists and the modern men—who say with us, "Amen. Man is dead." And thus perhaps it is easier to say this and be, in some sense at least, understood than it was fifty or a hundred years ago.

Second, there is physical death. A few short years, though Adam's life was longer than ours, and Adam's body will rot in the grave.

Third, there is eternal death in the penalty that is meted out. Those separated from God will ultimately "be punished with everlasting destruction from the presence of the Lord, and from the glory of his power" (2 Thess. 1:9). The end of the eating is not just the present situation as horrible and abnormal as it is, not just physical death, not just a blank, a vacuum. There is a horizontal extension—eternal death and eternal separation from the God who is really there—from his glory and his grace.

We must be careful to notice the loving provisions that God gave. Man was made in the image of God. God had told him that evil was possible, but man was good because he had not yet chosen evil. Man was in constant fellowship with God: "And they heard the voice of the LORD God walking in the garden" (Gen. 3:8). He was surrounded by a perfect environment, God himself having selected a special place for man himself within this creation: "And the LORD God planted a garden eastward in Eden; and there he put the man whom he had formed" (Gen. 2:8). Adam knew something of his place in history and he knew what Eve was: "And Adam called his wife's name Eve; because she was the mother of all living" (Gen. 3:20). The word *Eve* really means "living." Adam chose her name and in doing so showed that he knew who he was. Furthermore, man had a truly free choice with power to obey or to transgress. He was not (either materially or psychologically) deterministically conditioned. He was not programmed. Finally, it was a simple test and everything involved in it was made absolutely plain.

Enter the Serpent
We will begin to look now at a new stage in the flow of biblical history: "Now the serpent was more subtil than any beast of the field which the LORD God had made" (Gen. 3:10).

Immediately questions arise. We want to know more than we are actually given. So it is necessary for us to remind ourselves again just what kind of book the Bible is. As I have already indicated, the Bible is a book for fallen men. Wherever it touches upon anything, it does so with true truth, but not with exhaustive truth. That is, where it speaks of the cosmos, science, what it says is true. Likewise, where it touches history, it speaks with that I call true truth, that is, propositional, objective truth.

When the Bible talks about the supernatural world and tells us of heaven and things beyond this earth, they stand as corollaries to the theme of the book—the propositional communication in verbalized form from God to fallen man. The corollaries given are those we need to know to get the major thrust, the central purpose of the Bible. But it does not answer every question that we might ask about any of these matters. If everything concerning which we have a proper curiosity was given, the book would be larger than the great libraries of the world and no one could read through it all. John seems to have this thought in mind in the last verse of the Gospel of John: "And there are also many other things which Jesus did, the which, if they should be written every one, I suppose that even the world itself could not contain the books that should be written."

It is in this context that data concerning the supernatural world is given. We might well enjoy a book about the supernatural world. That half of the universe intrigues us, and it stands, not somewhere far off, but immediately before us almost as a fourth dimension so that there is indeed a cause-and-effect relationship between it and our own visible world at every existential moment. It really is not less natural and no less real than the seen part of the universe, and we cannot understand the seen half if we write off the existence of the unseen portion. But while we would be interested to find out some of these things in more detail, we are given adequate knowledge. Information about the supernatural world is brought in to help us

understand who we are as man, lost man looking for meaning and saved man looking toward the second coming of Christ. When the serpent enters, we are introduced to this other half of the universe.

One of the lies of Satan, by the way, is his attempt to convince us to follow modern liberal thought in breaking the Bible into pieces and destroying its unity. We recognize, of course, that while the Scripture is a whole it records an increasing revelation as time passes. But it all forms a unit and while we have increasing revelation we do not have contradictory revelation.

Interestingly enough, it is often toward the end of the Bible that clear explanations of earlier parts are given. By the time we study through the full circle of the whole book, we have what explanations we need, for now, of all the parts. Thus in Revelation we read this: "And the great dragon was cast out, that old serpent, called the Devil, and the Satan, which deceiveth the whole world: he was cast out into the earth, and his angels were cast out with him" (Rev. 12:9). It is unfortunate that the King James translation leaves out the definite article applied to Satan. One cannot translate *Satan* as a "general" adversary. Rather, he is "the" adversary, the Satan. He is the one who has deceived the whole world. But he is not alone; he has angels who are cast out with him. One is reminded of the flaming poetry of Milton who described Satan and his hosts so well. Along with Satan there were those who chose his way, those who joined his cortege, that leads not only to rebellion but to condemnation. Later in Revelation we are given further information: "And he [an angel] laid hold on the dragon, the old serpent, which is the Devil, and Satan, and bound him for a thousand years" (Rev. 20:2—ASV). Notice that this serpent is a special serpent. A definite article is used here again. You can call him the old serpent, or the devil, or the Satan. In any case, with this information before us, who we are dealing with in Genesis **79**

3:1 is clearly identified. The definite article that is applied to Satan in Revelation 12:9 and to the serpent in Revelation 20:2 and Genesis 3:1 is important. It has, in fact, been suggested that with the addition of the Hebrew definite article in Genesis 3:1 we have something called in Hebrew grammar an article of eminence. And if this is the case, the serpent actually is, even here, made a proper name—The Serpent.

Jesus tells us something significant about the devil when he challenges those who rejected Jesus while claiming to have God as their Father: "Ye are of your father the devil, and the lusts of your father ye will do. He was a murderer from the beginning, and abode not in the truth, because there is no truth in him. When he speaketh a lie, he speaketh of his own: for he is a liar, and the father of it" (Jn. 8:44). The point is that the devil does not abide, does not stand, in the truth. Rather, he is the liar behind all liars and stands in the lie back of all lies—that the creature can be equal with God. This was his own point of rebellion against his Creator, God. Every other lie is only an extension of this one. And this is who the devil is—the originator of The Lie.

This is the context, then, in which we should understand what I call the theology of the Fall. In Genesis we have a free man with an unprogrammed choice. And coming to this free man from the outside is the temptation of Satan. But we must go back even before this, and bind together Satan's fall and Adam's fall. Satan, without an outside temptation, had already chosen to revolt. He revolted from himself outward. Adam and Eve, on the other hand, were tempted by the father of The Lie, someone outside themselves. Although there is some debate over this, and without wishing to be dogmatic about it, I think that Isaiah 14:12-15 gives us the fall of Satan: "How art thou fallen from heaven, O Lucifer [that is, Day Star], son of the morning! how art thou cut down to the ground, which didst weaken the nations! For thou hast said in thine heart, I will ascend into heaven, I will exalt my throne above the stars of God: I will sit also upon the mount of the congregation, in the sides of the north: I will ascend above the heights of the clouds; I will be like the most High. Yet thou shalt be brought down to hell, to the sides of the pit."

Assuming that the word *stars* refers to the other angels, he was saying, in short, "I will be greater than all the rest." But he goes further, specifically adding, "I will *make myself* like the most High." Satan the liar, the originator of The Great Lie, in his heart (that is within himself, from himself outward) says, "I will be greater than the rest, and I will be equal with God."

The story of Satan in Isaiah is paralleled almost exactly in Genesis in regard to man's revolt. Satan wants to be equal with God, but the end of this is that he will be brought down into the abyss. In Genesis 3 the woman would be equal with God, but she ends in death. As we consider the entrance of the serpent into the garden, we see the revolt about to spread across the world of mankind which God has made. There is no revolt among the machines, nor the plants, nor the animals. But in the circle of that which can rebel, angels and men, we see rebellion.

I think it is clear that the devil used the animal, the serpent as his first try to challenge and defeat God in the world of mankind. In other words, The Serpent used a serpent. This is not the only time he himself employed Devil possession. In contrast to demon possession there are at least two other cases where the Devil himself used Devil possession.

Luke 22:3 tells us that at a crucial moment in the life of the Messiah (who had come to bruise The Serpent's head) Satan possessed Judas: "Then entered Satan into Judas surnamed Iscariot." Satan did not delegate this job to a second, but took it on himself. He entered into Judas.

The third place where there is a special effort on the part of Satan is yet to take place—at the time of the anti-Christ where one of anti-law will revolt against God. Revelation 13:4 portrays a tremendous picture of that future day when the forces of humanism—the united economic, religious and governmental forces—draw together in revolt, casting down the gauntlet before the God who is. Proud humanism is no longer naturalistic; it is joined to the acme of the occult. Under the reign of the anti-Christ, we read, "they worshipped the dragon (identified in Rev. 12:9 and 20:2 as Satan, *The Serpent*) which gave his authority unto the beast [anti-Christ]: and they worshipped the beast, saying, Who is like unto the beast? who is able to make war with him?" So Satan is here into the play again, completely committed to the struggle.

Returning to the third chapter of Genesis, we are not taken by surprise. Satan's use of something else, whether it be a Judas or an anti-Christ or a serpent, is not in any one of these cases unique.

The Temptation
With revolt already in the universe, with the angelic host split and a hierarchy of evil, the leader himself tempts Eve: "Yea, hath God said, Ye shall not eat of every tree of the garden?" (Gen. 3:1). The woman stands in her glory—the glory of being created in the image of God with no necessity upon her to choose evil. Standing in a perfect environment, having heard the voice of God, she is at a place where she can choose. What a wonder is man! Not mechanical man, not merely biological man, but man who can choose in a situation, as in the image of God, with no necessity upon him.

Satan comes to her and says, "Yea, hath God said, Ye

shall not eat of every tree of the garden?" What will she reply? "And the woman said unto the serpent, We may eat of the fruit of the trees of the garden: But of the fruit of the tree which is in the midst of the garden, God hath said, Ye shall not eat of it, neither shall ye touch it, lest ye die" (vv. 2-3). It has been pointed out that Eve added something here. God apparently had not said, "Don't touch it," but rather, "Don't eat it." I am not sure we should make much of this, but it should be noted. The serpent replies in a direct contradiction: "Ye shall not surely die" (v. 4). And the issue is joined.

But Satan offers something further: "For God doth know that in the day ye eat thereof, then your eyes shall be opened, and ye shall be as God, knowing good and evil" (v. 5). It is unfortunate that in the King James *God* is translated as plural, for it is not that they will be like some primitive gods, but that each of them will be like God himself. Notice the direct contradiction. God said in the day you eat you shall die; Satan said in the day you eat you will be like God.

In a way, there is a half truth here. Satan's approach has often taken that form ever since. It is true that Eve is indeed going to learn something. If she chooses to disobey and to rebel, she will have what she couldn't have otherwise—an experiential knowledge of evil and its results. So in a way Satan is telling her the truth. But what a useless, horrible knowledge! It is the knowledge of the child whose mother says, "Don't go near that fire, because if you do you will get hurt. You will catch fire and be burned." But the little child goes on in disobedience, falls into the fire and spends the next three days dying in agony. The child has learned something that it wouldn't have known experientially if it had listened to the knowledge given by its mother. But what a knowledge!

Eve's fall is not a fall upward but a fall downward in

every conceivable way. She already knows from the voice of God that "in the day you eat you will die." She can have experiential knowledge, but that knowledge is no truer knowledge than the knowledge from God, and the result is that the whole human race will be in agony.

It is a lie, of course, that she is going to be like God, because experiential knowledge of evil is not what makes God God. God is God because he is infinite, the non-dependent one. No created being will ever be able to be like him in this. Even in the area of knowledge, what Satan has said is a lie because God is infinite and knows all the possibilities, and he is not bound by limitedness. We, however, with all our knowledge are still bound by limitedness and always will be. So what Satan has said is a half truth but a total lie.

Eve's response is, first, to consider the situation: ". . . the woman saw that the tree was good for food, and that it was pleasant [a delight] to the eyes, and a tree to be desired to make one wise . . ." (v. 6). Three steps are involved: She looked at the tree and saw that it was good for physical food and that it was delightful to look at, and she desired the knowledge which would make her equal to God. Eve, with these things in her mind, is actually standing in the situation of the last commandment of the Ten Commandments: "Thou shalt not covet" (Ex. 20:17). After all the external commandments comes the commandment on which all the others rest. Coveting, wanting that which is not properly mine as I stand as a creature before the law of God, is really the basis of all sin, for it is the internal attitude which leads to the external breaking of the other nine commandments. This is what Paul had reference to in Romans 7:7 when he pointed out that the center of his own sin was coveting. Jesus also made it explicit in Matthew 5:21-22. He said that it isn't murder itself but the hatred that was in your heart first, ultimately leading to the murder, that stands at the heart of the issue. Likewise, he indicated in verses 27 and 28 that adultery is already there when it's only in one's mind. The internal later flows out into the external.

Eve stands exactly there—in the area of the internal where choices are always made. Paul in 2 Corinthians 11:3 hearkens back to her situation at a point of space-time history as he advises the church of his own day, "But I fear, lest by any means, as the serpent beguiled Eve through his subtilty, so your minds should be corrupted from the simplicity that is in Christ." We live in our thought life. This is who I am. And for Eve the choice was this: whether to remain as a creature or to try in rebellion to have what the finite creature can never have and to be what the finite creature can never be. And we hold our breath to see what Eve will choose in the inner man.

chapter 5

_____

**the space-time
fall and
its results**

Eve was faced with a choice, she pondered the situation
and then she put her hand into the history of man and
changed the course of human events.

The Fruit Is Eaten
The Genesis account is short and to the point: "And when
the woman saw that the tree was good for food, and that it
was pleasant to the eyes, and a tree to be desired to make
one wise, she took of the fruit thereof, and did eat, and
gave also unto her husband with her; and he did eat" (Gen.
3:6).[1] The flow is from the internal to the external; the sin
began in the thought-world and flowed outward. The sin
was, therefore, committed in that moment she believed
Satan instead of God. At this point the whole matter was
decided. Nonetheless, a history is involved, for first she
believed Satan, then she ate, and then she gave the fruit to
Adam.

Genesis 3:17 refers to this historical flow, for God in
speaking to Adam says that he has "hearkened unto the
voice of thy wife, and hast eaten of the tree." And we are
reminded, as we have seen in 2 Corinthians 11:3, that as
the serpent beguiled Eve through his subtlety (at her point
of history) so our own minds (at our point of history) may
also be corrupted from the simplicity that is in Christ.   **89**

Paul in 1 Timothy 2:14 points out something further: "And Adam was not deceived, but the woman being deceived was in the transgression." Temptation is extremely hard to resist when it is bound up with the man-woman relationship. For example, in Exodus 34:16 we are warned not to let the man-woman relationship lead us into idolatry (spoken of as going "a whoring after their gods").

Two great drives are built into man. The first is his need for a relationship to God, and the second his need for a relationship to the opposite sex. A special temptation is bound up with this sexual drive. How many young women are there who are faithful as Christians until they come to a certain age and feel with their whole being, without ever analyzing it, the need for marriage and are then swept over into marrying a non-Christian man? And how many men are there who are faithful until they feel the masculine drive and give up their faithfulness to God by marrying a woman who carries them into spiritual problems for the rest of their life? I look upon such young men and young women as I see them going through this, and I cry for them, because in a way there is no greater agony than suddenly to fall in love and then to realize that one must say no to this natural drive because it leads in that particular case to a severing of our greater relationship—our relationship to God. While what happened in the Garden of Eden was a space-time historic event, the man-woman relationship and force of temptation it must have presented to Adam is universal.

The Results of the Fall for the Human Race

The results of Adam and Eve's action are recorded in many places in Scripture, but nowhere more clearly than in Romans 5:12-19 where Paul emphasizes that Adam and Eve's action marked the entrance of sin into the human race. I will quote here part of this passage: "Therefore, as through one man sin entered into the world, and death through sin; and so death passed [spread] unto all men, for that all sinned:—for until the law sin was in the world; but sin is not imputed when there is no law. Nevertheless death reigned from Adam until Moses, even over them that had not sinned after the likeness of Adam's transgression, who is a figure of him that was to come. . . . For if by the trespass of the one the many died. . . . For if, by the trespass of the one, death reigned through the one. . . . So then as through one trespass the judgment came unto all men to condemnation. . . . For as through the one man's disobedience the many were made sinners . . ." (ASV).

The repetition makes the point obvious: By the action of one man in a historic, space-time situation, sin entered into the world of men. But this is not just a theoretical statement that gives us a reasonable and sufficient answer to man's present dilemma, explaining how the world can be so evil and God still be good. It is that in reality, from this time on, man *was* and *is* a sinner. Though some men do not like the teaching, the Bible continues like a sledge hammer, driving home the fact that evil has entered into the world of man, all men are now sinners, all men now sin. Listen to God's declaration concerning the human race in Jeremiah 17:9: "The heart is deceitful above all things, and desperately wicked: who can know it?"

Incidentally, in one way it is easier today than it was a few years ago to proclaim the sinfulness of man. On every side artists, novelists and protest singers are saying, "What's wrong with man? Something's wrong with man." The Bible agrees and gives us a realistic view of life: "The heart is deceitfully wicked."

I think the strongest words were spoken by Jesus himself in John 8:44, where he turns on those who are claiming the fatherhood of God and says: "Ye are of your father the devil, and the lusts of your father it is your will

91

to do" (ASV). In other words, Jesus is saying, "You choose to be in Satan's parade."

Isaiah writes, "All we like sheep have gone astray; we have turned every one to his own way" (Is. 53:6). It is obvious that if "all we like sheep have gone astray," I can no longer merely say *they* have gone astray, but I must say *I* have gone astray. I, too, sin. Paul picks this up in the letter to the Romans as he summarizes the status of all the races—first the Gentiles and then the Jews: "As it is written, There is none righteous, no, not one: There is none that understandeth, there is none that seeketh after God. They are all gone out of the way, they are together become unprofitable; there is none that doeth good, no, not one" (Rom. 3:10-12). If there is none that is righteous, no, not one, then I am included. I have written the word *me* in the margin of my Bible at this place. Galatians 3:10 carries the force: "For as many as are of the works of the law are under the curse: for it is written, Cursed is everyone that continueth not in all things which are written in the book of the law to do them." All mankind stands in this place. Not only the revealed law of God but also every moral motion of every man who has ever lived condemns men, because men keep neither the revealed law of God nor even live consistently according to their own moral motions. This is the point of Romans 2:1-2: "Therefore thou art inexcusable, O man, whosoever thou art that judgest: for wherein thou judgest another, thou condemnest thyself; for thou that judgest doest the same things. But we are sure that the judgment of God is according to truth against them which commit such things."

What Paul says involves the whole man as he comes to Scripture. The Bible never leaves this as a generalization or as an abstraction. Paul writes, "Therefore thou art inexcusable, O man." Perhaps the most important part of this

92 is that it is in the singular, for it speaks to every individual who hears or reads: "Whosoever thou art that judgest: for wherein thou judgest another, thou condemnest thyself; for thou that judgest doest the same things." The simple fact is that it is not only the man who has the written law of God, the Bible, who stands under the judgment of law, but every man who ever lived. I have pointed out elsewhere that wherever anthropologists and sociologists have been, they have found that men have moral motions. The specific standards may be different, but all men operate under moral categories. So Paul says here that a man stands condemned on the basis of his own moral motions, for every time he condemns another man he has put himself under the same condemnation. Every man makes moral judgments concerning other men and then does not keep them himself. The results? All men are sinners, and all men sin.

This indictment includes those who are now Christians as well as non-Christians. Men are not born Christians, a sort of special race. Every single man who is now a child of God was at one time a rebel. We are all hewn from the same rock, whether we come from a church background or a non-church background. No sacerdotalism can help man.

Am I a Christian today? Never forget, then, that yesterday I was as much a rebel as anyone who walks on the face of the earth. As Ephesians 2:2-3 says in burning words: "Wherein in time past ye walked according to the course of this world, according to the prince of the power of the air, the spirit that now worketh in the children of disobedience." He is talking here to the church at Ephesus. But he continues and adds himself to the list, he steps over and joins us, for it is not just "ye" but "we": "Among whom also we all had our conversation [meaning here our total way of life, our "life-form"] in the lusts of our flesh, fulfilling the desires of the flesh and of the mind; and were by nature the children of wrath, even as others." This is who we are. If we are Christians today, this is who we have been. We had a different king—the father of lies. We must not be proud, for as Ephesians 5:8 says, "For ye were sometimes darkness, but now ye are light in the Lord." Remember, you were also marked by Adam's sin, and you were sinners: "And you, that were sometime alienated and enemies in your mind by wicked works, yet now hath he reconciled" (Col. 1:21).

Don't be proud. As you look out across the world of sinners, weep for them. Be glad indeed if you are redeemed, but never forget as you look at others that you have been one of them, and in a real sense we are still one with them, for we still sin. Christians are not a special group of people who can be proud; Christians are those who are redeemed—and that is all!

Everywhere we turn we find the same thing: "For we ourselves [notice the "we" again] also were sometimes foolish, disobedient, deceived, serving divers lusts and pleasures, living in malice and envy, hateful, and hating one another" (Tit. 3:3). Paul never allowed those who followed his teaching to forget that they were not a special kind just because they may have been Jews at the beginning and circumcised or just because they were now baptized Christians. Each one must say, "I have been the rebel, I have been the sinner." The force of this is perhaps brought most fully in the great statement in 1 John 1:10: "If we say that we have not sinned, we make him [God] a liar, and his word is not in us." To forget in our emotional reactions as well as in our words that we indeed have been sinners, not only involved in the results of Adam's sin but deliberately sinning ourselves over and over and over again —to forget this is to call God a liar.

Thus, all men are under the judgment of God. Even the marvelous chapter that speaks so clearly of hope, the third chapter of the Gospel of John, twice emphasizes that men are under God's judgment. We read, for example, these words in John 3:18: "He that believeth on him is not condemned: but he that believeth not is condemned already, because he hath not believed in the name of the only begotten Son of God." The testimony of John the Baptist in the last verse of this chapter is even more emphatic: "He that believeth on the Son has everlasting life: but he that believeth not the Son shall not see life; but the wrath of God abideth on him" (v. 36). In a world that loves synthesis, the Bible stands with a message of total antithesis: He who believes has life *but* he who does not is subject to the wrath, the judgment, of God. Here, then, is the basic result of the space-time fall that we are considering in the flow of history—men are rebels and under the judgment of God.

Guilt before God

Other results of sin were immediately evident in the Garden of Eden: "And the eyes of them both were opened, and they knew that they were naked; and they sewed fig leaves together, and made themselves aprons" (Gen. 3:7). The word *aprons* in the Hebrew is interesting. Actually, it simply means to "gird yourself about," so people have translated the word in various ways. One Bible, the Breeches Bible of 1608, got its name from the way it translated this word. But whatever an *apron* is, it is something one puts around himself.

The significance is that Adam and Eve were brought to a realization of what they had done. They began to feel afraid and to feel guilt—and well they might, for their guilt feelings were rooted in true guilt. When a man has sinned against God, he not only has guilt feelings, he has true guilt; and he has true guilt even if he does not have feelings of guilt.

"And they heard the voice of the LORD God walking in   **95** the garden in the cool of the day: and Adam and his wife hid themselves from the presence of the LORD God amongst the trees of the garden" (v. 8). This is the verse we have used in our previous studies to indicate the wonder of the open communication which God had with man. In the garden in the cool (or the wind) of the day, there was open fellowship, open communion—open propositional communication between God and man before the Fall. But now that which was his wonder and his joy, the fulfillment of his need, an infinite, personal reference point with whom he could have communion and communication became the reason for his fear. He was going to meet God face to face! Once man had shaken his fist in the face of God, what had been so wonderful became a just reason for fear, because God was really there.

So we read: "And the LORD God called unto Adam, and said unto him, Where art thou? And he said, I heard the voice in the garden, and I was afraid, because I was naked; and I hid myself. And he said, Who told thee that thou wast naked? Hast thou eaten of the tree, whereof I commanded thee that thou shouldst not eat? And the man said, The woman whom thou gavest to be with me, she gave me of the tree, and I did eat. And the LORD God said unto the woman, What is this that thou hast done? And the woman said, The serpent beguiled me, and I did eat" (vv. 9-13).

The first thing we notice here is that Adam and Eve immediately begin to try to pass the guilt from themselves to another, and we have, therefore, the division which is at the very heart of man's relationship with man from this point on. The human race is divided—man against man. We do not have to wait for modern psychologists to talk about alienation. Here it is. Man is alienated from his wife—the wife from her husband—as they turn against each other, especially at the points of blame and guilt. All the alienation that any poet will ever write about is here already.

In a way, both Adam and Eve were right. Eve had given the fruit to Adam, and Satan had tempted Eve. But that does not shift the responsibility. Eve was responsible and Adam was responsible, and they stood in their responsibility before God.

God's Judgment on Man and Nature

As God speaks to the parties involved at this moment of history, we find four steps in his judgment of their action. First, he speaks to the serpent who has been used by Satan: "And the LORD God said unto the serpent, Because thou hast done this, thou art cursed above [*from among*] all cattle, and above [*from among*] every beast of the field; upon thy belly shalt thou go, and dust shalt thou eat all the days of thy life" (v. 14). As we shall see, all nature becomes abnormal yet the serpent is singled out in a special way "from among all cattle."

Second, in verse 15 he speaks to Satan; we will return to that.

Third, he speaks to the woman: "Unto the woman he said, I will greatly multiply thy pain [this is more accurate than the King James word *sorrow*] and thy conception; in pain thou shalt bring forth children; and thy desire shall be to thy husband, and he shall rule over thee." There are two parts here: the first relates to the womanness of the woman—the bearing of children—and the second to her relationship to her husband. In regard to the former, God says that he will multiply two things—not just the pain but also the conception. It seems clear that if man had not rebelled there would not have been as many children born.

In regard to the relationship to her husband, he says, "And thy desire shall be to thy husband, and he shall rule over thee." This one sentence puts an end to any pure democracy. In a fallen world pure democracy is not possi-

97

ble. Rather, God brings structure into the primary relationship of man—the man-woman relationship. In a fallen world (in every kind of society—big and small—and in every relationship) structure is needed for order. God himself here imposes it on the basic human relationship. Form is given and without such form freedom would only be chaos.

It is not simply because man is stronger that he is to have dominion (that's the argument of the Marquis de Sade). But rather he is to have dominion because God gives this as structure in the midst of a fallen world. The Bible makes plain that this relationship is not to be without love. As the New Testament puts it, the husband is to love his wife as Christ loved the church (Eph. 5:23). In a fallen world it is not surprising to find that men have turned this structure into a kind of slavery. It is not meant to be a slavery. In fact, it is in cultures where the Bible has been influential that the balance has been substantially restored. The Bible balances the structure and the love.

Nevertheless, it is still true: Since the Fall what God says in verse 16 is to be the structure or the form of the basic human relationship—the man-woman relationship. It is right that a woman should feel a need for freedom, a feeling of being a "human being" in the world. But when she tries to smash the structure of this basic relationship, finally what she does is to hurt herself. It is like unravelling the knot that holds the string of human relationships together. All other things flow from it—the loss of her own children's obedience and the crumbling of society about her. In a fallen world we need structure in every social relationship.

The Abnormal Universe
Fourth, God speaks to the man: "And unto Adam he said, Because thou hast hearkened unto the voice of thy wife,

and hast eaten of the tree, of which I commanded thee, saying, Thou shalt not eat of it: cursed is the ground for thy sake; in toil [the word *sorrow* in the King James is inaccurate] shalt thou eat of it all the days of thy life" (v. 17). In other words, at this point the external world is changed.

It is interesting that almost all of the results of God's judgment because of man's rebellion relate in some way to the external world. They are not just bound up in man's thought life; they are not merely psychological. Profound changes make the external, objective world abnormal. In the phrase *for thy sake* God is relating these external abnormalities to what Adam has done in the Fall.

All of these changes came about by fiat. Creation, as we have already seen, came by fiat. And, though we have come to the conclusion of creation with the creation of Eve, yet fiat has not ceased. The abnormality of the external world was brought about by fiat. Putting it into twentieth-century terminology, we can say this: The universe does not display a uniformity of cause and effect in a closed system; God speaks and something changes. We are reminded here of the long arguments that date back to the time of Lyell and Darwin concerning whether there could be such a thing as catastrophe—something that cut across the uniformity of cause and effect. Scripture answers this plainly: Yes, God spoke and that which he had created was changed.

So now the earth itself is abnormal. We read, for example, in Genesis 5:29, which speaks of the world before the flood: "And he [Noah's father] called his name Noah, saying, This same shall comfort us concerning our work and toil of our hands, because of the ground which the LORD hath cursed." The name *Noah* itself simply means rest or comfort. The Scripture says that at this point in the flow of biblical history men knew very well that the toil of their hands was a result of God's having changed the earth.

Why is it like this? Because, one might say, you, O unprogrammed and significant Adam, have revolted. Nature has been under your dominion (in this sense it is as an extension of himself, as a king's empire is an extension of himself). Therefore, when you changed, God changed the objective, external world. It as well as you is now abnormal.

It is interesting that in each of the steps of God's judgment toil is involved: The serpent goes upon his belly; the woman has pain in childbirth; the man has toil in his work.

Verse 18 continues: "Thorns also and thistles shall it bring forth to thee." The word *thistles* here means luxuriously-growing but useless plants. The phrase *it shall bring forth to thee* has in the Hebrew the sense of "it shall be caused to bud." This phrase, therefore, suggests that here, too, the change was wrought by fiat. Furthermore, the phrase suggests the modern biological term *mutation,* a non-sterile sport. That is, the plants had been one kind of thing and were reproducing likewise, and then God spoke and the plants began to bring forth something else and continue to reproduce in that new and different form.

The introduction of toil does not mean the introduction of work, because in Genesis 2:15, as we have seen, God took man and put him in the Garden of Eden "to dress it and to keep it." There was work before the Fall, but certainly we can see the force of the distinction before and after the Fall, in the language of Genesis 5:29, where labor is called the "toil of our hands, because of the ground which the LORD hath cursed." Since the whole structure of the external world has changed, the meaning of work has changed. Thus Genesis 3:19 says: "In the sweat of thy face shalt thou eat bread, till [the concept of "until" is important here] thou return unto the ground; for out of it

was thou taken: for dust thou art, and unto dust shalt

thou return."

The results are twofold. First, man shall have his food (and all else) by the sweat of his brow. Second, there is an end to this—an end that is not a release. The end is the greatest abnormality in the external world—the dissolution of the total man. A time will come at the end of each man's life when he physically dies and the unity of man— the unity of body and soul—is torn asunder. Christianity is not platonic; the soul is not considered all-important. Rather, at physical death that unity which man is meant to be is fractured. This is the second kind of death brought about by the Fall, the first being immediate separation from fellowship with God and the third being eternal death as men are judged in their rebellion and separated from God forever.

Christianity as a system does not begin with Christ as Savior, but with the infinite-personal God who created the world in the beginning and who made man significant in the flow of history. And man's significant act in revolt has made the world abnormal. Thus there is not a total un-broken continuity back to the way the world originally was. Non-Christian philosophers almost universally agree in seeing everything as normal, assuming things are as they have always been. The Christian sees things now as not the way they have always been. And, of course, this is very important to the explanation of evil in the world. But it is not only that. It is one way to understand the distinction between the naturalistic, non-Christian answers (whether spoken in philosophic, scientific or even religious language) and the Christian answer. The distinction is that as I look about me I know I live in an abnormal world.

Among contemporary philosophers Martin Heidegger in his later writings has suggested a sort of space-time fall. He says that prior to Aristotle, the pre-Socratic Greeks thought in a different way. Then when Aristotle intro- **101** duced the concept of rationality and logic, there was an epistemological fall. His notion, of course, has no moral overtones at all, but it is intriguing to me that Heidegger has come to realize that philosophy cannot explain reality if it begins with the notion that the world is normal. This the Bible has taught, but the Bible's explanation for the present abnormal world is in a moral Fall by a significant man, a fall which has changed the external flow of history as no epistemological fall could do. Heidegger's problem is that, while he well sees the need of a fall, he will not bow before the existence of the God who is there and the knowledge that God has given us. Hence he ends up with an insufficient fall and an insufficient answer.

Separations

Another way to look at the results of the Fall is to notice the separations that are caused by sin. First is the great separation, the separation between God and man. It underlies all other separations, not only in eternity but right now. Man no longer has the communion with God he was meant to have. Therefore, he cannot fulfill the purpose of his existence—to love God with all his heart, soul and mind—to stand as a finite personal point before an infinite-personal reference point and be in relationship with God himself. When man sinned, the purpose of his existence was smashed. And modern man is right when he says that man is dead. It is not that man is nothing, but that he is no longer able to fulfill his mannishness. Genesis 3:23-24 shows this separation between man and God in a real, historic, graphic sense.

As evangelicals we sometimes emphasize the first separation and fail to properly emphasize all the others that now exist. The second great separation is separation of man from himself. Man has fear. Man has psychological problems. How does a Christian understand these? Primarily as the abnormal separation of man from himself. Man's basic psychosis is his separation from God carried into his own personality as a separation from himself. Thus we have self-deception. All men are liars, but, most importantly, each man lies to himself. The greatest falsehood is not lying to other men but to ourselves. A related aspect is the loss of ability to acquire true knowledge. All his knowledge is now out of shape because the perspective is wrong, the framework is wrong. That is, man does not lose all his knowledge, but he loses "true knowledge," especially as he makes extensions from the bits and pieces of knowledge he does have.

Furthermore, man has separated his sexual life from its original high purpose as a vehicle of communication of person to person. Sexuality loses its personal dimension; men and women treat each other as things to be exploited. Finally, at physical death comes the separation of the soul from the body, the great separation of a man from himself.

The third of the great separations is man from man. This is the sociological separation. We have seen already how Adam was separated from Eve. Both of them immediately tried to pass off the blame for the Fall. This signals the loss of the possibility of their walking truly side by side in utopian democracy. Not only was man separated from his wife, but soon brother became separated from brother, Cain killing Abel. And, as we will see in the following chapter, there is a separation between the godly and the ungodly line of men. The godly line (those men who have returned to God) and the ungodly line (the unsaved humanity going on in rebellion) constitute two humanities. In one sense, of course, there is one humanity because we all come from one source. We are one blood, one flesh. But in the midst of one humanity, there are two humanities— the humanity that still stands in rebellion and the humanity that is redeemed.

Soon in the flow of history we come to the tower of Babel, and with it we have the division of languages. Modern linguistics has helped us to understand how great the issues are here. So much is involved with language. Then after the time of Abraham comes the division between Jew and Gentile. These separations (and others related to them) are like titanic sonic booms in the sociological upheavals coming down to, and perhaps especially in, our day.

The fourth separation is a separation of man from nature and nature from nature. Man has lost his full dominion, and now nature itself is often a means of judgment. There is, for example, the flood at the time of Noah and, of course, nature pitted against Job. The separation of man from nature and nature from nature seems also to have reached a climax in our day.

Man's sin causes all these separations between man and God, man and himself, man and man, and man and nature. The simple fact is that in wanting to be what man as a creature could not be, man lost what he could be. In every area and relationship men have lost what finite man could be in his proper place.

But there is one thing which he did not lose, and that is his mannishness, his being a human being. Man still stands in the image of God—twisted, broken, abnormal, but still the image-bearer of God. Man did not stop being human. As we have seen in Genesis 9:6 and in James 3:9, even after the Fall men are still in the image of God. Modern man does not see man as fallen, but he can find no significance for man. In the Bible's teaching man is fallen but significant.

Let us not be misled: Man is still man. The unsaved painter can still paint. The unsaved lover can still love. He still has moral motions. And, though twisted, the unsaved thinker can still think. And furthermore, he lives on after his own death. He doesn't just come to the end of his life and suddenly the clock stops. Man has meaning and significance. He may think that his history is just trash and junk, but it is not so.

Watch a man as he dies. Five minutes later he still exists. There is no such thing as stopping the existence of man. He still goes on. He has not lost his being as a human being. He has not lost those things which he intrinsically is as a man. He has not become an animal or a machine. And as I look out over the human race and see the lost—separated from God, separated from themselves, separated from other man, separated from nature—they are still men. Man still has tremendous value.

chapter 6

the two humanities

Division, separations—they rend the fabric of society. The history of man is the record of splits and schisms, every one of which has its origin in the primal separation of man from God. We turn now to some of the early forms which these separations took in the flow of biblical history.

Thy Seed and Her Seed
In Genesis 3:15 we have a rather different aspect of the curse that comes from Adam's rebellion. God here speaks to Satan who used the serpent: "And I will put enmity between thee and the woman, and between thy seed and her seed; he shall bruise thy head, and thou shalt bruise his heel" (ASV). It is important to emphasize that the seed here is considered personal, "he." The one who is promised here is a person. A person will bruise Satan's head, and in doing so will be wounded.

Let us reflect further on *thy seed and her seed*—the seed of the serpent and the seed of the woman. The reference to "her seed" is peculiar in Semitic languages because as in our own thinking the male is considered the one who has the seed. Descent is indicated in men as in animals as the descent or offspring of the male. Why is it different here? Is it possible that this way of speaking already cast a shadow of the Virgin Birth? Does it suggest that when the Messiah was born, he would be the seed of the woman and   **109** that in his conception there would be no male seed?

Another implication of Genesis 3:15 is indicated in Hebrews 2:14. Speaking of Jesus, the writer of Hebrews says, "Forasmuch then as the children are partakers of flesh and blood, he [Jesus] also himself likewise took part of the same; that through death he might destroy him that had the power of death, that is, the devil." Here is an indication that Jesus fulfilled the promise in Genesis 3:15, for it is the Messiah who is to be bruised, and yet, in the bruising, destroy the power of death and the devil. By this death, he would "deliver them who through fear of death were all their lifetime subject to bondage" (v. 15). That is, there would be a substitutionary note to his death face to face with the adversary, Satan, and by this death the results of the Fall would be overcome. There is also a tie between Genesis 3:15 and Hebrews 2:13 that I think is not just coincidental—the phrase, *I and the children which God hath given me.* The chief thrust is undoubtedly on the substitutionary aspect of Jesus' death. Yet it also reminds us of that magnificent passage in Isaiah 53:10: "Yet it pleased the LORD to bruise him; he hath put him to grief: when thou shalt make his soul an offering for sin, he shall see his seed, he shall prolong his days, and the pleasure of the LORD shall prosper in his hand." Note again: *He shall see his seed.* It is in this sense, therefore, that God has given Jesus children. Romans 16:20 also ties in with Genesis 3:15. Speaking to the Christians in Rome, Paul writes, "And the God of peace shall bruise Satan under your feet shortly." The reference is to the second coming of the Lord Jesus Christ when God himself shall bruise Satan under the feet of the Christians.

Therefore, we find that indeed Christ *is the seed* of the woman in Genesis 3:15. And yet from his unique redemptive work he *has a seed* which shall stand against the seed **110** of Satan. And when we bring these together, I think we can feel the force of what is gradually developed through Scripture beginning from this phrase in Genesis 3:15. Christ is to be the second Adam and the second founder of the race.

We remember that in theological terms Adam lived under the covenant of works. That is, he could approach God without any mediator. He did not need a Savior. Soteriology would not have existed in Christian theology if there had been no Fall. Adam stood before God under the covenant of works. Then, when Jesus came, Jesus worked. He continued and finished the work under the covenant of works. Because of the Fall and our own sinning, we can no longer come to God under this covenant. But Christ finished the work needed for us in his substitutionary death, and in doing so he became the second Adam—the second founder of the human race.

Two Suits of Clothes

In Genesis 3:7 we learn that Adam and Eve found out that they were "naked" and so they "sewed fig leaves together and made themselves aprons." That is, immediately after their rebellion as they came face to face with what had previously been their great joy and their great fulfillment —themselves in open communion with God—they were now afraid and tried to cover themselves. But in verse 21 God took this covering away and gave them a coat of skins: "Unto Adam also and to his wife did the LORD God make coats of skins, and clothed them." Probably these were the first animals to die. This indicates, I believe, that man could not stand before God in his own covering. Rather, he needed a covering from God—a covering of a specific nature—a covering that required sacrifice and death, a covering not provided by man but by God. One would want to be careful not to press this into a dogma, but it is my opinion that this was the beginning of the Old **111**

Testament sacrificial system looking forward to the coming of the one who would crush Satan's head. If this is so, God himself provided this picture, in the same way that, in the reality which this pictures, the Father in his love sent the Son.

We might note at this point that the death of Jesus Christ was not an afterthought in history. It isn't that sometime, say, around 100 B.C. God said, "What shall we do about this?" and then suddenly the idea of the death of Christ dawned on him. Rather, 1 Peter 1:19-20 and other passages indicate that the death of Christ, "the precious blood of the Christ, as of a lamb without blemish and without spot," was "foreordained before the foundation of the world." Thus the death of Christ in space and time, planned before history began, the solution of man's rebellion in the light of God's character of holiness and love, stood in the natural flow of all that had been.

The Ultimate Separation

We recall that numerous separations came about because of the Fall. There were alienations between God and man, man and himself, man and other men, man and nature, and nature and nature. The last separation is the separation between the Father and the Son when Jesus died on the cross. The separations that resulted from man's Fall were brought to their climax as Jesus, the second person of the Trinity, being bruised and bearing our sins in substitution, cried aloud: "My God, my God, why hast thou forsaken me?" (Mt. 27:46).

In such a setting as this, we are ready to grasp the full impact of the verses in Romans which we considered only partially in the previous chapter. I will quote the whole section this time (Rom. 5:12-21) and from the American Standard Version (1901) in order to make the passage clearer.

Therefore, as through one man sin entered into the world, and death through sin; and so death passed unto all men, for that all sinned:—for until the law sin was in the world; but sin is not imputed when there is no law. Nevertheless death reigned from Adam until Moses, even over them that had not sinned after the likeness of Adam's transgression, who is a figure of him that was to come. But not as the trespass, so also is the free gift. For if by the trespass of the one the many died, much more did the grace of the one man, Jesus Christ, abound unto the many. And not as through one that sinned, so is the gift: for the judgment came of one unto condemnation, but the free gift came of many trespasses unto justification. For if, by the trespass of the one, death reigned through the one; much more shall they that receive the abundance of grace and of the gift of righteousness reign in life through the one, even Jesus Christ. So then, as through one trespass the judgment came unto all men to condemnation; even so through one act of righteousness the free gift came unto all men to justification of life. For as through the one man's disobedience the many were made sinners, even so through the obedience of the one shall the many be made righteous. And the law came in besides, that the trespass might abound; but where sin abounded, grace did abound more exceedingly: that, as sin reigned in death, even so might grace reign through righteousness unto eternal life through Jesus Christ our Lord.

It is clear that Christ is the second Adam, the second founder of the human race. He picks up the covenant of works at the place where Adam forfeited it. As Lazarus Spengler wrote so long ago in 1524:

As by one man all mankind fell
And, prone to sin, then faced hell,

> So by one Man, who took our place,
> We now are sure of God's grace.
> We thank thee, Christ; new life is ours. . . .

This is exactly what was promised in Genesis 3:15: "And I will put enmity between thee and the woman, and between thy seed and her seed; he shall bruise thy head, and thou shalt bruise his heel" (ASV). Already we have the death of Christ in promise—the first promise—made immediately after the rebellion and the Fall. The death of Christ, therefore, is presented as the solution to all the separations of which we spoke.

By the sufficiency of the death of Christ, these separations will be perfectly healed at his second coming. And yet the Bible says that (in the present life) on the basis of the shed blood of the Lord Jesus Christ, through faith and in the power of the Holy Spirit, there is to be substantial healing in regard to all these separations. Sir Francis Bacon (1561-1626) pointed this out in *Novum Organum Scientiarum.* I've quoted this in some of my other books, but it fits here as well: "Man by the Fall fell at the same time from his state of innocence and from his dominion over nature. Both of these losses, however, can even in this life be in some part repaired; the former by religion and faith, the latter by the arts and sciences." This is to be the Christian view of life. A Christian, understanding the abnormality of nature, can see the arts and the sciences substantially delivered under God. And he can see even in this life a substantial reparation of the division between man and nature which one day, at the second coming of Jesus, will be perfect and complete.

Therefore, in the flow of history as we come to Genesis 3:15 we see that (except for Christ's work) the covenant of works is past. From this time on the covenant of grace applies. From here to the last man who will ever pass from death to life, man no longer can come in his own works. It is well to put it in the first person singular: I cannot come by my own works. I can come only through Christ's finished work. I can come only on the basis of the covenant of grace, the benefits of which I now receive as a free gift.

We can say this in a different way. Prior to the Fall, Adam in coming to God only had to bow once—as a creature before the Creator. But now, after the Fall of Adam, we must bow twice—as a creature before the Creator and as a sinner coming to a holy God through Jesus' work.

Acceptable and Unacceptable Worship

So far in our study of the flow of history we have covered two major steps: the situation in the beginning when all was good and the introduction of the abnormality brought about by the Fall. Our third major subject is acceptable and unacceptable worship after the Fall.

In Genesis 4:1 we read: "And Adam knew Eve his wife; and she conceived, and bare Cain, and said, I have gotten a man from the LORD." Here is the first baby to be born. What a wonder it must have been for Eve suddenly to have in her hands a little baby from her own body. Imagine her amazement as she looked at it: "Why, yes, it's just like Adam! I have gotten a man from the Lord!"

We wonder if she could possibly have had in mind the promise in Genesis 3:15. There is no way to be sure, of course. But do you suppose she said to herself, "Maybe this is the one who will bring the solution to the problem we introduced"? As Christians living on this side of the New Testament, we think of the contrast to Mary to whom the seed of the woman was really born in the Virgin Birth. In Hebrews 12:24 the writer is speaking to men living after the time of Jesus, reminding them that they have come "to Jesus the mediator of the new covenant, and to the blood of sprinkling, that speaketh better things than that of Abel." In Genesis 4:10 God said that Abel's **115** blood was calling out concerning the fact that Cain had killed him. It was the cry of the first murder, brother killing brother, a part of the separation because of the Fall. Christ's blood is the solution.

But in Genesis 4:1 Eve has just given birth to Cain! So if she had in mind that this was the one who was to solve the problems of the Fall, how wrong she was! Born naturally, he brings forth the results of the fallen human race. A savior? No, he is going to kill his brother. What a contrast between the first-born child and Christ!

In Genesis 4:2 we have the birth of the second child: "And she again bare his brother Abel." As the two grow up, we are brought to the question of acceptable and unacceptable worship this side of the Fall: "And in process of time it came to pass, that Cain brought of the fruit of the ground an offering unto the LORD. And Abel, he also brought of the firstlings of his flock and of the fat thereof. And the LORD had respect unto Abel and his offering: But unto Cain and to his offering he had not respect. And Cain was very wroth, and his countenance fell" (vv. 3-4).

Hebrews 11:4 tells us what was involved: "By faith Abel offered unto God a more excellent sacrifice than Cain." The distinction is that Abel's act of sacrifice was *by faith*.

The whole process is related to Romans 4 which gives the clearest possible description of such faith: "Abraham believed God, and it was counted unto him for righteousness" (Rom. 4:3). This is God's description of faith—the very opposite of a Kierkegaardian leap into the void, God gave for Abraham a specific, propositional promise and Abraham believed God. This belief was reckoned unto him for righteousness. In other words, Abraham's faith involved content.

How much content Abel had we do not know, but then we should be conscious of the fact that the Bible does not

tell us how he knew how to bring an offering at all. And

this is not unusual; in the book of Genesis information has often been given that we do not know has been given until someone acts on it—for example, the clean and unclean beasts at the time of Noah (Gen. 7:2) or Abraham and the tithe (Gen. 14:20). So here it is clear that Abel did have knowledge about offerings even though the Bible has not told us when this knowledge was given. We could wonder if Abel's parents had told him of the promise of Genesis 3:15 and the skins. And while this would be only speculation, one thing is not speculation: From this time onward, sacrifice was known and practiced, and the New Testament ties this up with the sacrifice of Christ.

We can hardly forget the words of John the Baptist, who (while he is recorded in the New Testament) is the last Old Testament prophet. When Jesus was just appearing on the public scene, one of the gospel writers recorded this: "The next day John seeth Jesus coming unto him, and saith, Behold the Lamb of God, which taketh away the sin of the world" (Jn. 1:29). You will notice that John the Baptist gives no explanation. He doesn't need to, because the Jews understood the Old Testament emphasis at this particular point.

In 1 Corinthians 5:7 Paul calls Christ our Passover in the same way, expecting understanding without explanation. The book of Hebrews repeatedly draws the parallel of the death of Christ and the Old Testament sacrifices. For example, Hebrews 7:26: "For such an high priest became us, who is holy, harmless, undefiled, separated from sinners, and higher than the heavens: Who needeth not daily, as those high priests, to offer up sacrifice, first for his own sins, and then for the people's: for this he did once for all when he offered up himself." And, as we have already seen, Revelation 5:11-12 refers to Jesus as the Lamb of God who has been slain and is therefore worthy to receive the power and the glory.

The Historicity of Cain and Abel

Just as in the case of Adam and Eve, the New Testament considers Cain and Abel as characters in history. We read in 1 John 3:12: "Not as Cain, who was of that wicked one, and slew his brother. And wherefore slew he him? Because his own works were evil, and his brother's righteous." Jude 11 repeats this: "Woe unto them! for they have gone in the way of Cain. . . ." But notice that, while in both cases the historicity of Cain is assumed, more than a historic fact is involved. In the flow of history, there is a *line of Cain* in which we should not walk. In contrast, in Hebrews 11:4 Abel is put in a line of historic characters, the line of faith, and we are commanded to walk in this line. More than this, Abel is the first one named in this line, and so in a real way this could be called the *line of Abel.*

The way of Cain is contrasted with the way of Abel, and that contrast is introduced in Genesis 4:6-7: "And the LORD said unto Cain, Why art thou wroth? and why is thy countenance fallen? If thou doest well, shalt thou not be accepted? And if thou doest not well, sin lieth at the door. And unto thee shall be his desire, and thou shalt rule over him." Some take the possible reading of *sin offering* rather than *sin* to be the proper reading here. But, while the detail of the translation of these verses may be discussed, the central thought is definite. God is saying, "Why is your countenance fallen, Cain? You can still be accepted. You've made a mistake, but there is a way out." It seems to me that God is telling Cain to go back and do what he should have done in the first place. By picking up the thread of acceptable worship, he could stop the rebellion (as far as he himself was concerned) right there. Instead he did something else: "And Cain talked with Abel his brother: and it came to pass, when they were in the field, that Cain rose up against Abel his brother and slew him" (v. 8). Instead of going back and doing what would have been right, he did something overwhelmingly wrong.

From here on two lines spread out before us—the way of Cain and the way of Abel. As we have pointed out, a separation between man and man had come as soon as Adam and Eve each tried to shift the blame from himself. But the separation is now accentuated with contrast between acceptable and unacceptable worship. From here on there are two humanities—the humanity that comes to God, bowing twice, and the humanity that follows in the way of Cain. The separation between man and man now extends to the separation between brothers. The love which should have existed between them as fellow beings created by God in the image of God has now become hatred and murder.

It is interesting that this murder sprang up, as we are told in the New Testament, exactly at the point of not believing God: One believed God, one didn't.

"And the LORD said unto Cain, Where is Abel thy brother? And he said, I know not: Am I my brother's keeper? And he said, What hast thou done? the voice of thy brother's blood crieth unto me from the ground" (Gen. 4:9-10). The blood of Abel speaks and cries for judgment and justice, and this cry echoes right down into the book of Revelation where we find the martyrs saying, "How long, O Lord, holy and true, dost thou not judge and avenge our blood on them that dwell on the earth?" (Rev. 6:10).

Abel's blood cries out, "Judgment! Judgment!" And God must judge because he is a holy God. If he shrugged his shoulders and walked away, there would be no moral absolute in the universe. Hebrews, fortunately, gives us further dimension. There is another way, one rooted in the blood of Jesus shed in history. This blood "speaketh better things than that of Abel" (Heb. 12:24). The blood of Jesus goes beyond justice and offers mercy. It cries "Salvation!" **119** on the basis of Jesus' death to all who will hear.

The Culture of the Ungodly Line

Genesis 4:11-24 tells of the gradually developing culture of the ungodly line. For man is still really man, and he can bring forth a culture. But it is a culture with a mark upon it, a culture without the true God.

We need to note here, in passing, that verses 11-24 do not constitute a chronology any more than do the genealogies of the godly line which begin at verse 25. Rather, these passages exactly fit the literary form found in all parts of Genesis: The unimportant aspects (in this case the ungodly line) are quickly gotten out of the way so that the more central aspects (the godly line) might be dealt with in detail. We do not, therefore, know how much time elapses before we come to verse 24. It is not necessary that verse 24 contain history that precedes that in verse 25, for verse 24 brings to a close the consideration of the ungodly line, and verse 25 picks up the godly line.

Verses 23 and 24 are a perfect description of the ungodly, humanistic culture of all generations: "And Lamech said unto his wives, Adah and Zillah, Hear my voice; ye wives of Lamech, hearken unto my speech: for I have slain a man for wounding me, and a young man for my hurt." Or to paraphrase this: "Because a man wounded me, I paid him back. I just killed him." Look at what Lamech did! Isn't that terrific? "O you wives, listen to me, both of you: This fellow hit me. I fixed him. I killed him." "If Cain is avenged sevenfold, truly Lamech seventy and sevenfold." Here is humanistic culture without God. It is egoism and pride centered in man; this culture has lost the concept not only of God but of man as one who loves his brother.

The Culture of the Godly Line

Genesis 4:25 takes up the godly line: "And Adam knew

his wife again; and she bare a son, and called his name Seth: For God, said she, hath appointed me another seed instead of Abel, whom Cain slew." Seth, therefore, takes the place of Abel as the vehicle of the godly line. "And to Seth, to him also there was born a son; and he called his name Enos: then began men to call on the name of the LORD." Or possibly "Men began to call themselves *by the name of the Lord.*" In other words, at this particular place the godly line marks itself with the name of God in exactly the same way as Christians later were marked by the name of Christ. Both marked themselves by the name of the one they followed.

We learn, by the way, from Genesis 5:3 that when Seth was born, Adam was 130 years old. Therefore, there was not a great deal of time between the creation of man and the Fall, because all the way up to the time of the birth of Seth only 130 years had passed.

In conclusion, I would make three points. First, Adam and Eve had thrown away the opportunity to come to God on the basis of the covenant of works. From then on the only way men could come to God was on the basis of the covenant of grace. It was not that there was no work involved in this covenant, but that the work was Christ's not man's. This is true whether, as in the Old Testament, men looked forward to the work of Christ to come in history (the promise becoming known in increasing detail as time passed), or whether, as in our case, we look back to the death of Christ as the Savior in history.

Therefore, since Cain, everyone in the world stands either in the place of Cain or the place of Abel. From this time on in the flow of history there are two humanities. The one humanity says there is no God, or it makes gods in its own imagination, or it tries to come to the true God in its own way. The other humanity comes to the true God in God's way. There is no neutral ground.

Second, as far as the promise in Genesis 3:15 is concerned, the Messiah could have come from anywhere in the human race. But Seth brings the first narrowing of the promise. From this time on, the Messiah will come from his line.

Third, when we look at Cain killing Abel, we can see a horrible lack of the love which should have existed between men as equal creatures—not just because they were fleshly brothers, though this makes the matter sharper, but simply because they were equally created by God. They were of the same flesh, the same blood, of one kind, of one race. In contrast to Cain, we who are Christians and therefore stand as the seed given to Christ in his substitutionary work are to show in the present life the restored brotherhood in restored love. This is the Christian's calling. We are to show the opposite of what Cain, that murderer, showed. If we have become the second humanity, if we have come indeed under the blood of the second founder of the race, the second Adam, men should look at us as we stand in the midst of the seed of the line of Cain and they should see a reversal of Cain's attitude. This should be true not just in our simple acts but in our whole culture.

The Bible makes plain who stands among this brotherhood. In Matthew 12:47-50 Jesus' natural mother and his natural brothers came as he was talking to the people. "Then one said unto him [Jesus], Behold, thy mother and thy brethren stand without, desiring to speak with thee." But Jesus points out that the merely physical relationship is not central: "Who is my mother? and who are my brethren? And he stretched forth his hand toward his disciples, and said, Behold my mother and my brethren! For whoever shall do the will of my Father which is in heaven, the same is my brother, and sister, and mother." Here then is the brotherhood. The same thing is made evident in Matthew 23:8 where Jesus instructs his disciples, "But be not ye called Rabbi: for one is your Master, even Christ; and all ye are brethren." Thus a new humanity is established on the basis of the work of Christ, and this new humanity is to love the brotherhood as brothers, and all men as neighbors.

We have long known that men were to live in a loving relationship with each other. As 1 John 3:11-12 says, "this is the message [or commandment] that ye heard from the beginning, that we should love one another." John is saying that this commandment dates not just from Moses but from the time when God created men to be men. "Not as Cain, who was of that wicked one, and slew his brother": Here is the contrast. We are called as Christians to step out from the line of Cain and to reverse that line. The world should be able to look upon us and see a love that stands, first of all, among the brotherhood but also extends (as commanded in the story of the good Samaritan) to all men.

Evangelism is a calling, but not the first calling. Building congregations is a calling, but not the first calling. A Christian's first call is to step from the line of Cain into the line of Abel, upon the basis of the shed blood of the Lamb of God, to return to the first commandment to love God, to love the brotherhood, and then to love one's neighbor as himself.

Abraham was a man of faith, a man of God, who in a specific way is a perfect example of standing in the line of Abel in contrast to the line of Cain. Facing Lot, his nephew, at a crucial time in a difficult relationship which had developed between them, Abraham said, "Let there be no strife, I pray thee, between me and thee, and between my herdmen and thy herdmen; for we are brethren" (Gen. 13:8). Abraham stood in precisely the place where all those who have become children of God should stand. And notice that there was a cost to doing so. Abraham said to

123

Lot, "Is not the whole land before thee? separate thyself, I pray thee, from me: if thou wilt take the left hand, then I will go to the right; or if thou depart to the right hand, then I will go to the left." Abraham paid a tremendous price. He stood in complete contrast to Cain. He gave the first choice of grazing land to a younger man. Abraham in costly love stood in the spirit of the godly line. In every age and every situation this is the Christian's place.

chapter 7

**Noah
and the
flood**

History flows on, the course having been set by Adam and
Eve and humanity divided by Cain and Abel. The history
of divided humanity develops from the two lines delineated in Genesis 4:16-24 (the line of Cain) and Genesis
4:25–5:32 (the line of Seth). In the account which follows these genealogies, we are introduced to a world in
which moral decay comes to so permeate society that only
one man is left in the godly line. But this puts us ahead of
our story.

"And He Died"
Throughout Genesis 5, which begins by recapitulating the
heritage of the line of Seth, emphasis is placed on the
conclusion of each man's life. Verse 5, in reference to
Adam, ends, "and he died." Verses 8, 11, 14, 17, 20, 27
and 31, in reference to Seth, Enos, Cainan, Mahalaleel,
Jared, Methuselah and Lamech, also end, "and he died."
Thus, as we run through this genealogy, we are reminded
over and over that we live in an abnormal world; since man
has revolted things are not the way God made them originally. But there is a curious exception to the phrase *and he
died.* Verse 24 comments, "And Enoch walked with God:
and he was not; for God took him." Both verses 22 and 24
contain that first phrase *and Enoch walked with God,* indicating that Enoch was indeed a man of God. The same   **127**

phrase is used with reference to Noah in Genesis 6:9. But with Enoch something else is special: "He was not; for God took him."

Hebrews 11:5 gives us further information: "By faith Enoch was translated [*taken up*] that he should not see death; and was not found, because God had translated him: for before his translation he had this testimony, that he pleased God." A similar *translation,* Elijah's, is explained in more detail in 2 Kings 2. Enoch and Elijah stand out as unique, being taken to God without dying.

Genealogy and Chronology

Genesis 5 raises a very interesting question. What is the connection between this Old Testament genealogy and chronology? Before the turn of the century, Professor William Greene at Princeton Theological Seminary and Professor Benjamin B. Warfield following him maintained that the genealogies in Genesis should not be taken as a chronology. And, while much of their scholarship had to be a response to liberal theology's attack on biblical history, I think that the understanding that these genealogies are not a chronology is obvious from Scripture itself.

First, the relationship between the sequence of names and chronology is not always a straight line. In Genesis 5:32 we read, "And Noah was five hundred years old: and Noah begat Shem, Ham, and Japheth." It would appear from this passage that Shem is older than Ham who is older than Japheth. But in Genesis 9:24 we are told that "Noah awoke from his wine, and knew what his *youngest* son had done unto him" (ASV). The reference is to Ham. Likewise, anyone reading Exodus 2 would certainly feel that Moses was the oldest son. Nevertheless, we learn in Exodus 7:7 that his brother Aaron was actually three years older. Consequently, the content of these various passages are accurate, but chronology was not what the authors had

noah and the flood

in mind. Undoubtedly Shem was named first because he was the most important one in the flow of biblical history. What they were recording *was* the flow of history—the thing we are talking of in this book—the flow of origins, especially of the Jews, for whom such things were of great importance, as we shall see in a moment. The Bible does not mislead us. It indicates that the genealogies are not chronological.

A second reason why we must not take genealogy for chronology is that several passages make it obvious that the writers knew the chronology but that they still deliberately omitted several steps in the genealogy. For example, if we compare 1 Chronicles 6:3-14 with Ezra 7:2, we find Ezra, despite the fact that he was a scribe and surely would have known all of the steps, omitted names in the genealogical tree. Not only this, but he seems to have added two names omitted in the 1 Chronicles genealogy. Of course, some of these men may have been known by more than one name as was common in Old Testament history, and there is a possibility of a later scribe's error. Nonetheless, it does seem that some names were consciously omitted by Ezra.

An even more startling case which shows what the Jewish people were doing with their genealogies occurs in 1 Chronicles 26:24. Here we read, "And Shebuel the son of Gershom, the son of Moses, was ruler of the treasures." The time is that of David, roughly 1000 B.C., and the issue is that Shebuel had an official position on the basis of his genealogical line. The intriguing thing is that Gershom is the first-generation son of Moses, and yet between him and the next man, Shebuel, stand at least 400 years. There is no doubt that we have here a tremendous gap in years and in intervening generations. Thus we are reminded that the purpose of all this is to indicate the flow of official, historic lines. It is important to say, "This man comes from

129

such and such an origin."

Another clear case is found in Matthew's genealogy of Christ. In Matthew 1:8 we read, "And Asa begat Jehoshaphat; and Jehoshaphat begat Joram; and Joram begat Uzziah" (ASV). Yet if we go back into the Old Testament we will find that Uzziah's father, grandfather and great-grandfather are omitted in Matthew's genealogy. (See 1 Chron. 3:11-12; in this list Uzziah is called Azariah.) The important point is that Jesus is to be seen in the right genealogical line, and after that has been accomplished, chronology is of little or no interest.

Prior to the time of Abraham, there is no possible way to date the history of what we find in Scripture. After Abraham, we can date the biblical history and correlate it with secular history. When the Bible itself reaches back and picks up events and genealogies in the time before Abraham, it never uses these early genealogies as a chronology. It never adds up these numbers for dating.

There is a third reason why it should be quite obvious that these genealogies are not meant to be a chronology. If they were, it would mean that Adam, Enoch and Methuselah were contemporaries, and that just doesn't seem to fit at all. If this were the case the silence of the Bible in regard to these interrelationships would seem curious. But the situation is even more striking after the flood, because in this postdiluvian era if genealogy were chronology, all of the postdiluvians, including Noah, would have still been living when Abraham was 50 years of age. That would seem to be impossible. Furthermore, Shem, Salah and Eber would all have outlived Abraham, and Eber would still have been living when Jacob was with Laban. The simple fact is that this does not fit into the rest of biblical history. We will consider this further when we take up Genesis 10—11, but at this particular place we can say very clearly

130 that the Bible does not invite us to use the genealogies in

Scripture as a chronology.

The Sons of God and the Daughters of Men
Genesis 6:1-2 raises a question which men have discussed
for many years: "And it came to pass, when men began to
multiply on the face of the earth, and daughters were born
unto them, That the sons of God saw the daughters of men
that they were fair; and they took them wives of all which
they chose." The difficulty is with the phrase *the sons of
God* because this phrase can mean either of two things: (1)
the godly line, those who were calling themselves by the
name of the Lord (as in Genesis 4:26) or (2) the angels (as
in Job 1:6). What has stirred men's curiosity is that the
book of Jude seems to refer to this. Verses 6-7 read, "And
angels that kept not their own principality, but left their
proper habitation, he hath kept in everlasting bonds under
darkness unto the judgment of the great day. Even as
Sodom and Gomorrah, and the cities about them, having
in like manner given themselves over to fornication and
gone after strange flesh [the Greek says *other flesh*], are
set forth as an example, suffering the punishment of eternal fire" (ASV). This passage seems to say that there are
angels who left their own proper place and are specifically
under judgment because they acted like the people of
Sodom and Gomorrah. That is, as the people of Sodom
and Gomorrah sought "other flesh" in homosexuality,
these angels sought flesh that was "other flesh"; they involved themselves with human women in what could be
called fornication.

There is further interest along this line if one understands this as a co-mingling of the angelic and the human,
for then it is possible that it was the original historic
source of an element common in mythology. More and
more we are finding that mythology in general though
greatly contorted very often has some historic base. And **131**

the interesting thing is that one myth that one finds over and over again in many parts of the world is that somewhere a long time ago supernatural beings had sexual intercourse with natural women and produced a special breed of people.

Such a notion is further strengthened by Genesis 6:4: "There were giants [Nephilim] in the earth in those days; and also after that, when the sons of God came in unto the daughters of men, and they bare children to them, the same became mighty men which were of old, men of renown." One can speculate, therefore, that the mighty men which were of old, men of renown, might be the historic reality behind these myths.

The other reading—that verse 2 denotes that there were those in the godly line who intermarried with others in the ungodly line to the destruction of the godly line—fits into the whole of Scripture, for there is a constant prohibition throughout the Old and New Testaments against the people of God marrying those who are not of the people of God. The Old Testament says repeatedly: If you marry those who are not God's people, and if you give your sons and daughters to them, the godly line will be destroyed. The New Testament contains the same command: "Be ye not unequally yoked together with unbelievers: for what fellowship hath righteousness with unrighteousness? and what communion hath light with darkness?" (2 Cor. 6:14). This passage has to do with those links which are central to men's lives, and no link is more central than marriage. This point is made explicit in the great marriage passage in 1 Corinthians 7:39. Paul instructs the church that "the wife is bound by the law as long as her husband liveth; but if her husband be dead, she is at liberty to be married to whom she will; *only in the Lord*." The principle is clear: God's people are to marry God's people.

132   It is, therefore, possible to interpret Genesis 6:2 as indi-

cating the intermarriage between the godly line and the
ungodly line.

One Man Left in the Godly Line
Genesis 6:5-12 brings us to a point in history where there
is only one man left in the godly line:

And God saw that the wickedness of man was great in
the earth, and that every imagination of the thoughts
of his heart was only evil continually [the Hebrew
reads, *every day*]. And it repented the LORD that he
had made man on the earth, and it grieved him at his
heart. And the LORD said, I will destroy man [blot
out man] whom I have created [note again this word
created] from the face of the earth; both man, and
beast, and the creeping thing, and the fowls of the air
[not the fishes, because in the form of destruction,
the flood, of course, fish can live]; for it repenteth
me that I have made them. But Noah found grace in
the eyes of the LORD. These are the generations of
Noah: Noah was a just man and perfect in his generation, and Noah walked with God. And Noah begat
three sons, Shem, Ham, and Japheth. The earth also
was corrupt before God, and the earth was filled with
violence. And God looked upon the earth, and, behold, it was corrupt; for all flesh had corrupted his
way upon the earth.

We might ask, "Isn't it strange that only one man is left
in the godly line?" But, surely, Scripture points out that
this is the general course of every era. Man's heart is in
rebellion against God, and the rebellious heart must be
taken into account in balance with the factor of a sufficient knowledge of God. In each era the case is similar. For
example, by the time of Abraham, the world had thrown
away almost all of its knowledge of the true God. Likewise, by the time of Christ, the Jews had so turned from **133**

God that only a minority accepted their Old-Testament-prophesied Messiah. And we are amply warned that the end of our own era will be exactly the same. Because of the rebellion of man's heart the course is not upward. Therefore, speaking of the end of our age, Jesus could say, "When the Son of man cometh, shall he find faith on the earth?" (Lk. 18:8). As we shall see shortly, Jesus expressly connects the time of Noah with the time of his second coming.

"These Are the Generations"

Genesis 6:9 uses a phrase which is one of the striking literary forms of Genesis: "These are the generations of . . . ." In verse 9 the reference is to Noah, but the phrase has already been used in Genesis 2:4 and 5:1. It is, in fact, used eleven times in Genesis.

In 1936 Wiseman suggested that the phrase *these are the generations of* is not the beginning but the end of a section. The phrase means "this is (has been) the story of . . . ." As he pointed out, the tablets of that time put such a title at the bottom rather than at the top. Thus, for example, in Genesis 2:4, "These are the generations of the heavens and of the earth" would summarize that which had already been given. This would be likewise true of Genesis 5:1: "This is the book of the generations of Adam." Wiseman suggested that Moses had other materials in front of him when he wrote the book of Genesis and that he incorporated them. This is only speculation but it is interesting, for if this were so then the inspiration would be in the choice of the material used. It would be parallel to Hezekiah's men copying out the proverbs of Solomon (Prov. 25:1).

In any case, Genesis is without question broken into sections signaled by these phrases. There is, first, the **134** cosmic creation ("these are the generations of the heavens and of the earth"—Gen. 2:4), second, the period of Adam ("this is the book of the generations of Adam"—Gen. 5:1), third, the period of Noah ("these are the generations of Noah"—Gen. 6:9), and fourth, the era of Noah's sons ("these are the generations of the sons of Noah, Shem, Ham, and Japheth"—Gen. 10:1). This phrase also occurs in Genesis 11:10; 11:27; 25:12; 25:19; 36:1; 36:9; 37:2. This phrase is a literary form that gives unity to the whole book of Genesis.

The Building of the Ark
The generation we are concerned with now, however, is Noah's. In Genesis 6:13-15 we find God warning Noah, telling him to escape the coming judgment: "And God said unto Noah, The end of all flesh is come before me; for the earth is filled with violence through them; and, behold, I will destroy them with [*from* or *with respect to*] the earth. Make thee an ark of gopher wood; rooms [it should be translated more like *a place to rest* or *nest*] shalt thou make in the ark, and shalt pitch it within and without with pitch. And this is the fashion which thou shalt make it of: The length of the ark shall be three hundred cubits, the breadth of it fifty cubits, and the height of it thirty cubits."

There are two things to notice in this section. First, the plan of the ark was not dreamed up by Noah. He was not a boat engineer. Rather, the plan of the ark derived from God himself. It was a specific, propositional revelation that dealt with detail. At another great moment when the tabernacle was to be built God also gave the specific plans and dimensions of all that concerned it (Ex. 25:9-40).

God says to Noah, "A tremendous judgment is coming and here is the way to escape. Build a huge boat." It's interesting that among the common myths in the world's history, no other one is so widespread as the story of the **135** flood. From China to the American Indians and even the pre-Colombian Indians, one finds in strange forms the myth of the great flood. Most of these myths have weird elements—foolish elements, for example the descriptions of the boat that was used. In the Bible these strange and foolish elements are not there. We would say, then, that the Bible gives us the history of the flood; the myths all over the world are contorted, but show that men everywhere have a memory of it. Here in the Bible is the one flood story whose details, including the construction of the vessel, are reasonable.

If we assume that a cubit is 18 inches (one cannot be absolutely sure), we can calculate that the ark would contain 1,518,750 cubic feet—quite a boat! The deck area of the three stories would total 101,250 square feet. Furthermore, a boat with the dimensions given is floatable. It just so happens, in fact, that the size of this ark is almost exactly the size of the *Great Eastern* which laid the first North Atlantic cable. Hence, compared to the various myths and other stories of the flood throughout the world, this one bears the mark of history.

The New Testament, of course, insists that the flood and the Noah account are history. Hebrews 11:7 reads: "By faith Noah, being warned of God of things not seen as yet, moved with fear, prepared an ark to the saving of his house; by which he condemned the world, and became heir of the righteousness which is by faith." Notice again, just as with Abel in Hebrews 11:4 and Abraham in Romans 4:3, faith is related to a propositional promise from God. Noah could not yet see the flood, but he had a propositional statement that judgment was to come, and he was told in a most propositional statement the dimensions of the boat he was to build. And he was asked to build a boat somewhere with no adequate water in sight:

This was his act of faith—believing a propositional promise

of God.

More striking yet is the parallel which Jesus drew between his own future space-time coming and the flood in the past. Jesus emphasizes that his future second coming is a historic event, "But of the day and hour knoweth no man, no, not the angels of heaven, but my Father only. But as the days of Noe were, so shall also the coming of the Son of man be" (Mt. 24:36-37). The word translated *coming* used throughout the New Testament in relation to Christ's second coming means *presence.* It is "a being alongside of," that is, there is coming a future time when Jesus will be present on the earth—historically, space-time present in the same way as he was on earth when he spoke these words. Jesus continues, "For as in the days that were before the flood they were eating and drinking, marrying and giving in marriage, until the day that Noe entered into the ark, And knew not until the flood came, and took them all away; so shall also the coming [here again *presence*] of the Son of man be. Then shall two be in the field; the one shall be taken, and the other left. Two women shall be grinding at the mill; the one shall be taken, and the other left" (vv. 38-41).

The parallel is interesting even in detail, for it takes up the normality of life upon the earth before the flood came and parallels it with the normality of life just before Jesus comes. Just as life was going along in an unbroken line and the flood came, so life will be going on in an unbroken line and the first step in the second coming of Christ will occur.

Many other passages speak clearly of the historicity of the flood. Isaiah 54:9 records God as saying, "For this is as the waters of Noah unto me: for as I have sworn that the waters of Noah should no more go over the earth; so have I sworn that I would not be wroth with thee, nor rebuke thee." That is, God is saying that his promise is as sure as **137** the events concerning the historic fact of the flood. Likewise, 1 Peter 3:20 says in a parenthetical way, ". . . the longsuffering of God waited in the days of Noah, while the ark was a preparing, wherein few, that is, eight souls were saved through water" (ASV). The specificity of the number, eight, underscores the fact that the event was considered historical. Furthermore, 2 Peter 2:5 speaks about God who "spared not the old world, but saved Noah the eighth person [that is, eight people, Noah and seven others], a preacher of righteousness, bringing in the flood upon the world of the ungodly." Notice another historic detail: Noah was a preacher of righteousness. This, by the way, is the text which some Christians have used to picture Noah preaching as he built the ark; that's really an extension of the text but seems warranted. Noah didn't just build a boat in faith resting on the warning of God; he also preached righteousness.

In 2 Peter 3:3-7 the flood is again paralleled to the second coming of Christ. Prior to the time when Jesus is to come, there will be scoffers who will say, "Where is the promise of his coming? for since the fathers fell asleep, all things continue as they were from the beginning of the creation." To paraphrase this in twentieth-century language: "Where is the promise of his coming? There has been an absolute uniformity of natural causes in a closed system. Why are you talking about something catastrophic? It's always been like this, and we say it's going to keep on being like this." Peter explains this reaction: "For this they willingly are ignorant of, that by the word of God the heavens were of old, and the earth standing out of the water and in the water: Whereby the world that then was, being overflowed with water, perished: But the heavens and the earth, which are now, by the same word are kept in store, reserved unto fire against the day of judgment and perdition of ungodly men." Thus past historical events in the time of Noah are paralleled with coming historical events.

But there is a further note here—a note of universality. If the judgment at the second coming of Christ is taken to be universal, isn't the judgment by water at the time of Noah also universal? Christians who love the Scripture have discussed at length whether the flood was universal or not. I believe it was, but I do not think by any means that we should make it a "test of orthodoxy." We cannot base a case on the word *earth* in Genesis 7:4 ("every living substance [thing] that I have made will I destroy off the face of the *earth*"), because the word can be translated "ground." Rather, the argument for universality rests on other factors, including the parallel between the second coming of Christ and the flood as it is given in the New Testament passages we have just considered. The tone of the language that is used in Genesis suggests this as well. It seems to have a totality about it, the same kind of thrust as Genesis 1—a thrust conveying universality. For instance, in Genesis 7:23 we read, "And every living thing was destroyed [*blotted out*] that was upon the face of the ground, both man, and cattle, and the creeping things, and birds of the heavens; and they were destroyed [*blotted out*] from the earth: and Noah only was left, and they that were with him in the ark" (ASV). That sounds universal. Furthermore, the word *ground* (as it appears in both the American Standard Version and the King James translation of this verse) and the word *earth* in this verse are two different words in Hebrew. Admittedly, both can be more limited; but the fact that two different words are used may add some weight to the argument in favor of universality with regard to the flood. Also in Genesis 7:23 the other living things are closely paralleled to men, and Genesis 9:19 and 10:32 make it absolutely certain that Noah and his family were the only men left. That the **139** flood was universal as far as man is concerned is made totally final in the Scripture.

Another difficulty arises if the flood is not universal, and I don't see how anyone can quite get around this factor. If a flood occurs in a limited area, a lot of animals can be drowned but not all of them. There is no way you can eliminate them all unless they are all in a sealed canyon. When a forest fire or flood comes, the animals take off.

One further indication that the flood was universal is found in God's statement after the flood is over: "And I will remember my covenant, which is between me and you and every living creature of all flesh; and the waters shall no more become a flood to destroy all flesh" (Gen. 9:15). Unless the flood were universal and did in fact destroy all animals on the earth, I don't understand how to interpret the phrase *the waters shall no more become a flood to destroy all flesh.* Of course, this does not include the fish. The promise does not preclude smaller floods, nor does it preclude the possibility that the world could be destroyed by fire. The covenant is, however, specific: No flood will again destroy all flesh.

The Date of the Flood

We have already pointed out that since the genealogies do not constitute a chronology, we cannot date the flood. There are reasons to think that, if the dating systems used in present anthropological studies are correct, the flood should be dated *before* 20,000 B.C. Let me say that I think these dating systems are still open to question, but *if* they are correct, then this date is to be considered. If all men but Noah and his family were destroyed (Scripture clearly states this), then the flood would have had to occur sometime before this date. Most anthropologists estimate that the American Indians entered America from the

Orient in about 20,000 B.C. across either an ice bridge or a land bridge over the Bering Strait. Thus, because the Indians were descendants of Noah and his sons, the flood would have had to be prior to this time. It is interesting that both the North American Indians and the pre-Colombian Indians of South America had flood myths.

Noah Enters the Ark
If we take the various New Testament passages and put them together with the Old Testament material, we see that while Noah was building the ark he was preaching and that there was the normal flow of life just like that on any day today. We hear cars on the road, people are in the village, people are in the city, others are farming, some people are making their dinners, there's a couple making love, a baby being born and life is moving on in its general stream. This is exactly the picture that the Bible gives of the situation immediately before the flood.

Then, when the ark was built, God said to Noah, "Of every clean beast thou shalt take to thee by sevens, the male and his female: and of beasts that are not clean by two, the male and his female. Of fowls also of the air by sevens, the male and the female; to keep seed alive upon the face of all the earth" (Gen. 7:2-3). As we have seen, it is apparent that Noah already had a knowledge from the past, a knowledge which the Bible does not record as being given at a specific point, because Noah needed no explanation of the difference between "clean" and "unclean." Such a knowledge with regard to clean and unclean is also assumed in Genesis 8:20. This fact is interesting because it means that these men may very well have known considerably more than we think.

Finally, it comes time for Noah and his retinue to go into the ark, for God says, "For yet seven days, and I will cause it to rain upon the earth forty days and forty nights; **141** and every living substance [*thing*] that I have made will I destroy from off the face of the earth" (Gen. 7:4). Genesis 7:10 says, "And it came to pass after seven days, that the waters of the food were [*came*] upon the earth." God is saying to them, "Now the ark is finished; you've been preaching here, but that is over. You're to go into the ark and stay there for seven days." I believe that to follow this command called for very strong faith on Noah's part.

Remember, the boat is out on dry land. We don't know the altitude at which it was built, but it would be something like having an ocean liner in Huemoz. What a strange sight! People are people and psychology is psychology. You can imagine them coming up and poking at the boat and, to put it mildly, being skeptical. The black preachers in America used to weave tremendous stories of Noah preaching as he built and people coming by, standing before the boat and laughing. Of course, it's a stretch of the imagination, and yet it must have been strange to get into this boat and then just sit there for seven days.

What a picture of Christian faith this is! It is not that there are no propositional promises; it is not that there are no good and sufficient reasons to know that the things are true. But faith is standing against what is seen at the moment and being willing to be out on the end of a limb in believing God. It's not a leap; it's not a denial of rationality. But it is sitting in this boat out in the middle of Huemoz when most people say it just doesn't make sense. If any generation has ever been in this situation, it's ours. We are surrounded by a total, monolithic consensus that says to us, "It doesn't make sense; it is against the uniformity of cause and effect in a closed system!"

Genesis 7:7 expressly says that there were eight people: "And Noah went in, and his sons, and his wife, and his sons' wives with him, into the ark, because of the waters of the flood." There is an interesting parallel here to the destruction of Sodom and Gomorrah (Christ himself draws it) in that a whole family was involved in one man's faithfulness. Thus we find that not only Lot was brought out, but those daughters who would listen to his warning in Sodom. Likewise, there is a parallel with the Passover, because, when the Jews killed their Passover beast in Egypt, and put the blood on the door, both the first-born in the family and the first-born of the animals in the Jewish house were protected from death.

Verses 11 and 12 are a parenthesis covering the whole forty-day period. Verse 11 says, "In the six hundredth year of Noah's life, in the second month, the seventeenth day of the month, the same day were all the fountains of the great deep broken up, and the windows of heaven were opened." Surely this is an insistence on history. The genealogies are not meant to be a chronology, but the Bible dates this event in detail in regard to the central character of the event.

Verse 11 also tells us there were two sources of water which opened up—the fountains of the great deep and the windows of heaven. The water came from two sources—"the windows of heaven" and the "fountains of the great deep." The water involved was something more than forty days of rain. Verse 11 could cover a wide field of possibilities.

The flood is thus presented as catastrophic, not necessarily in the flow of the uniformity of cause and effect we know now. Furthermore, 2 Peter 3:3-7 parallels the catastrophic flood to the future catastrophic destruction by fire.

Modern man believes in a uniformity of natural causes in a closed system, and therefore such a thing as a catastrophe in the sense of an abrupt change is not considered possible. John Woodward (d. 1772), the father of the study of fossils, made plain that he held the concept of **143** orderly procedure and catastrophe, that is, that there could be great breaks. Just a little over a century ago Charles Lyell began to insist on uniformity as opposed to catastrophe. The concept of catastrophe in general was thrown away, especially in geology. And with it the creation account and the flood account were rejected.

Today, interestingly enough, geologists are finding it necessary to bring catastrophe (though they usually do not use this term) back into the story, for they have not been able to demonstrate that everything (in the order of events we know today) flows in a simple cause-and-effect line.

We must remember that the Christian position does not deny cause and effect. Rather, as I have stressed in my other books, it was the Christian base that gave a reason to expect cause and effect, orderly procedure. It is the concept of cause and effect in a closed system which is at issue. God has not made himself a prisoner to the machine of the universe. He can act into it. And consequently, a Christian, whether he is considering a great catastrophe such as the flood or something less dramatic, does not have to choose between a random universe without cause and effect and a universe of cause and effect in a closed system. God is a living God and can work into the machine at any time he wants to.

There are many problems for those who reject the catastrophic. Any events which do not fit the order of events we know today give difficulty. For example, science is wrestling with a great mystery involving a curious event that happened about 10,000 B.C. in what is now the Arctic. I am referring here, of course, to the frozen mammoths and other animals. As far as we can tell, for the past 12,000 years this area has been uniformly cold. But, as is obvious from the study of these great mammoths and the other animals that have been found there, up to that time

144 it had been warm. When the animals froze, they died so quickly that plants of a warmer climate were still in their mouths, neither spit out nor swallowed.

Nobody can explain this—nobody. This is a matter of science that has nothing to do with the Bible, and I am not trying to relate it to the flood. I think it probably occurred after the flood. Nevertheless one cannot say that the idea of a great catastrophe is stupid. These great beasts were frozen with such rapidity that the meat was still good to eat when it was found. Scientists who are familiar with deep-freezing have figured out that on the basis of the mass of these huge animals, the temperature would have had to drop within a few hours to -150° F. Nobody knows how or why this happened.

The point is that we can discuss such things as the flood and still be giving honest answers to honest questions. There is no reason for a Christian to be defensive just because he is surrounded by men whose framework is the uniformity of natural causes in a closed system and who have arbitrarily given up the notion of catastrophe.

God Shuts the Door

Genesis 7:16 is a striking verse: "And they that went in, went in male and female of all flesh, as God had commanded him: and the LORD shut him in." This is a hard verse, and I am thankful that Noah did not have to shut the door. Knowing that men would soon be drowning all around him, I don't see how Noah could have done it. But he wasn't asked to. He was asked to be faithful—a preacher of righteousness. He was asked to believe God and God's propositional promise. He was asked to build a boat. But after he built the boat, the time came when God shut the door. That was the end of the time of salvation. It was closed because God had closed it at a point in the flow of history.

In the rest of the seventh chapter, then, the destruction **145** comes. God's judgment falls against sin, for God is holy and there are moral absolutes and we live in a moral universe. If God does not hate and judge sin, then he is not a holy God, there are no moral absolutes and we do not live in a moral universe. But the whole Bible resounds with emphasis: God does hate sin and God will judge sin. There comes a day when God shuts the door.

We have already seen the parallel between the judgment that God brought upon the men of Noah's day and the judgment which is to come at the second coming of Christ. Genesis 6:5 and Matthew 24:37-38 are in many ways parallel passages. Both times are times when man stands in total revolt, times of great wickedness, and men in both days are unaware until destruction overtakes them: "For as in the days that were before the flood they were eating and drinking, marrying and giving in marriage, until the day that Noe entered into the ark. And knew not until the flood came, and took them all away; so shall also the coming of the Son of man be. Then shall two be in the field; the one shall be taken, and the other left. Two women shall be grinding at the mill; the one shall be taken, and the other left" (Mt. 24:38-41). Jesus draws a conclusion from this: "Watch therefore: for ye know not what day [this is the correct translation] your Lord doth come" (v. 42). And lest we miss the point, Jesus repeats it: "Therefore be ye also ready: for in such an hour as ye think not the Son of man cometh" (v. 44). Jesus is saying you do not know what day (v. 42) and you do not know what hour (v. 44).

This judgment does not come only to the open pagans. One parable indicates that some even within the church are really not God's people. Jesus concludes, "Watch therefore, for ye know neither the day nor the hour wherein the Son of man cometh" (Mt. 25:13). A time of judgment does arrive. This is the flow of history.

chapter 8

**from
Noah to
Babel
to Abraham**

As the ark comes to rest, a new era in the history of man
begins. Again from a unified beginning (in the family of
Noah) the course of man's history runs to divisions—the
divisions of Babel, for example—and yet man comes closer
to the time when the basic divisions of man will be healed.

The Ark Comes to Rest
In Genesis 8:2 we read, "The fountains also of the deep
and the windows of heaven were stopped, and the rain
from heaven was restrained." That is, both sources of the
flood water were shut off. "The ark rested in the seventh
month on the seventeenth day of the month, upon the
mountains of Ararat" (v. 4). Ararat, as mentioned in 2
Kings 19:37, Isaiah 37:38 and Jeremiah 51:27, is the land
of Armenia. Assyrian documents likewise speak of the
kingdom of Ararat. It is not a mythical land by any means,
but one that is well known in both past and present history.

Throughout chapters 7 and 8 a very careful chronology
is recorded: "This happened on such a day, and that happened on such another day." The warp and woof of space-
time history continue to be woven. Thus, there was a time
when the ark came to rest and a geographical point at
which it happened in the land of Armenia.

Another sort of corroboration for the historical nature   **149** of this event occurs in Genesis 8:7-9: "And he sent forth a raven, which went forth to and fro, until the waters were dried up from off the earth. Also he sent forth a dove from him, to see if the waters were abated from off the face of the ground; But the dove found no rest for the sole of her foot, and she returned unto him into the ark, for the waters were on the face of the whole earth: then he put forth his hand, and took her, and pulled her in unto him into the ark." The form of the narrative gives the impression that something really occurred. It doesn't sound like a myth or a story.

There is, for example, a notable difference between the account here and the epics of Homer. In Homer the characters have little psychological depth. Erich Auerbach in *Mimesis* stresses the contrast between the Bible's presentation and that of Homer. He says that the heroes in Homer's epics arise each morning as if it were the first day that the world began, while the biblical account has a valid, psychological depth which emphasizes historicity. In reading the Bible we do not feel that we are dealing with cardboard situations, and this passage in Genesis 8:7-9 is a good example of this.

We read that Noah put out his hand and he "caused the dove to come in unto him in the ark" (this is more accurate than the King James rendering). Then the dove is sent out again: "And he stayed yet other seven days; and again he sent forth the dove out of the ark; And the dove came in to him in the evening; and, lo, in her mouth was an olive leaf pluckt off: so Noah knew the waters were abated from off the earth" (vv. 10-11). This is one of those biblical events that men keep as a symbol even after they quite openly say they no longer believe the Scripture. The dove with an olive branch in its mouth is universally used to signify peace. Incidentally, too, it is another indication that people are ignorant if they do not know the facts of the Bible, for so many of these symbols assume a comprehension that derives from the Scripture itself.

When Noah had learned that the waters had abated, he "removed the covering of the ark" (v. 13). This is a sharp contrast to Genesis 7:16 where we read that when Noah had entered the ark, "the Lord shut him in." God shut the door, sealed it and closed the possibility for further entrance. But Noah himself was able to open it when the right moment came. Then God specifically commanded that Noah go out from the ark, and he did so (vv. 15-19).

Noah's Sacrifice

When Noah had come forth from the ark, he made a sacrifice: "And Noah builded an altar unto the LORD; and took of every clean beast, and of every clean fowl, and offered burnt offerings on the altar" (Gen. 8:20). As we have pointed out, we constantly come to situations in the Old Testament, especially in Genesis, where men have knowledge that we would not expect them to have. In other words, God has taught them things that are not recorded in Scripture. We cannot assume that just because a certain knowledge is not recorded in Scripture that we can make an absolute negative that they did not have such knowledge.

The Life Is in the Blood

It is in chapter 9 that we first find God specifically giving the animals to man for food: "And God blessed Noah and his sons, and said unto them, Be fruitful and multiply, and replenish the earth. And the fear of you and the dread of you shall be upon every beast of the earth, and upon every fowl of the air, upon all that moveth upon the earth, and upon all the fishes of the sea; into your hand are they delivered. Every moving thing that liveth shall be food for you; even as the green herb have I given you all things" **151**

(Gen. 9:1-3). At the time of Noah, therefore, God expressly said that meat was open to them for food. It was all
right for them to eat the flesh of animals.

But there is a limit: "But flesh with the life thereof,
which is the blood thereof, shall ye not eat" (v. 4). Blood,
as is shown in the later writings of Moses, specifically in
Leviticus, is tied up with the life of the animal and it is
reserved for atonement. They were commanded to be careful at that point.

Likewise, we see why God commands capital punishment: "And surely your blood of your lives will I require;
at the hand of every beast will I require it, and at the hand
of man; at the hand of every man's brother will I require
the life of man. Whoso sheddeth man's blood, by man shall
his blood be shed: for in the image of God made he man"
(Gen. 9:5-6). God commands capital punishment simply
because of the unique value of that which the murderer
has killed. When a man is murdered, an image-bearer of
God is killed. Man continues after the Fall to be in the
image of God, and that makes murder heinous indeed.
Modern man who relates himself to the machine and to the
animal does not really understand the tremendous stature
of man and therefore he sees no reason why murder is
inherently different from any other crime.

Capital punishment was, however, not to be admin-
istered carelessly. For example, we could consider God's
commands concerning the cities of refuge as the Jews came
into a new land and became a state there (Num. 35:9-34;
Josh. 20:1-9). A careful distinction was made between premeditated murder and a mistake or an accident. In the case
of a clearly demonstrated premeditated murder, a man
commits a serious crime because he has taken it in his own
power to destroy a unique and tremendous being—one that
stands as qualitatively and not just quantitatively different
from all else.

A New Step in the Covenant Relationship

So far in our study we have covered two steps in the covenant relationship, the covenant promises of God to fallen man. The first, in Genesis 3:15, though not explicitly referred to as a covenant, is certainly a promise. It was a promise made to man concerning the coming solution of the problems which derive from man's rebellion against God. The second step occurs in Genesis 6:18-19 as God is talking to Noah: "But with thee will I establish my covenant; and thou shalt come into the ark, thou, and thy sons, and thy wife, and thy sons' wives with thee. And of every living thing of all flesh. . . ." That is, God is saying, "With you and with every living thing I will establish my covenant." It is worth noting that this is the covenant which God in Isaiah 54:9 refers to as parallel to a further covenant he is making with the Jews. That is, God points back to the covenant with Noah that he made in history in order to stress the certainty of further promises to the Jews that he is making in history at a later time.

Let us examine the Noahic covenant in some detail. First, it is an everlasting covenant. "And the bow shall be in the cloud; and I will look upon it, that I may remember the everlasting covenant between God and every living creature of all flesh that is upon the earth" (Gen. 9:16).

Second, it is established both with Noah and his descendants (vv. 9, 11-12) and with "every living creature" (vv. 10-12, 16). God is making a covenant not only with man who can understand it but with the beasts who cannot understand it. Verse 13 generalizes it even further: "I do set my bow in the cloud, and it shall be for a token of a covenant between me and the *earth*."

If we remember what we saw in Romans 8:19-23 concerning God's promises with regard to all creation at the time of the second coming of Christ, God's care of all creation in his covenant here in Genesis will not take us by **153** surprise. It is a part of the total scriptural framework.

The sign that marks the covenant with Noah is the rainbow (v. 13). Sometimes it is assumed that the Bible suggests that rainbows had never existed before. There is no reason why this needs to be the case. For one thing, later on there are two other signs given to mark covenant promises—circumcision in the case of Abraham and baptism in the case of Christians. But neither of these two tokens was new. They had been used by many people before and were simply given a Jewish or a Christian meaning—a definite meaning from God himself. This may, therefore, be true for the rainbow as well. God may simply have given it a new meaning. It is possible, however, that completely new physical conditions existed after the time of the flood and that the rainbow was a new thing. The Bible does not tell us, and either way would fit what these verses say.

Each of the covenant signs is appropriate, the rainbow specifically contrasting with circumcision, the covenant sign given to Abraham. The latter was a sign in man's body and was totally appropriate because man alone was involved; it marked an individual as one of the covenant people. Here, however, more than man is involved, and so the sign is not given in the body of Noah but in the sky, that which "covers" the whole of that to which the covenant applies—man and the rest of creation as well. Consider the aptness of the sign of baptism in the New Testament. In the Old Testament the father in a special way worshipped for the whole family, and thus the covenant sign of circumcision was appropriate. In the New Testament the wall of partition was broken down, and women as well as men now come directly to God, worshipping equally and immediately before him. Hence, the covenant sign of baptism is appropriate.

154   Often at L'Abri we have long discussions about the fact

that man, if he is only rationalistic, cannot really be sure that the sun is going to rise tomorrow morning; all he has is statistics and averages. The Christian can be sure. His certainty is not only based upon the observation of ten million sunrises, but on the total structure that gives a sufficient answer and, in that structure, the promise of God. As long as the earth goes on in the era in which we are, we can be sure of this: The sun will rise and the sun will set and the seasons will come in their natural and proper place. For this is the promise of God: "While the earth remaineth, seedtime and harvest, and cold and heat, and summer and winter, and day and night shall not cease" (Gen. 8:22).

A New Step in the Messianic Prophecy

The first Messianic prophecy is Genesis 3:15, that the seed of the woman shall bruise the serpent's head. A specific woman will be involved, but the promise, as far as its application is concerned, is as wide as the whole human race. Later it becomes clear that this one who will fulfill Genesis 3:15 will come through the line of Seth and not through the line of Cain. And in the present passage, Genesis 9:26-27, we see a further detailing: "And he said, Blessed be Jehovah, the God of Shem; and let Canaan be his servant. God enlarge Japheth, And let him dwell in the tents of Shem" (ASV). In other words, the promise that was first given to all men is now narrowed to the Semitic peoples. The Semitic peoples are a large group, related by language, living in what we now call the Near East. Yet, these verses in Genesis make plain that though the promise will be fulfilled through the Semitic people, it is actually open to the whole human race. It is simply that the Semitic people will be the channel—the cradle, as it were— the conduit out of which the whole of mankind will have a blessing.

Genealogy Not Chronology

Chapter 10 again brings us to the genealogies, and as we have said before, the genealogies themselves make it evident that their purpose is not chronology. For example, Genesis 10:2 speaks of a man bringing forth countries: "The sons of Japheth; Gomer, and Magog, and Madai, and Javan, and Tubal, and Meshech, and Tiras." Gomer, Magog, Tubal—these are countries. Verse 4 depicts a man as bringing forth peoples. This is clearer in the Hebrew where the *îm* endings indicate the plural. God is saying, "Do you want to know the flow of history? It's the flow of history that is important, and this is it." In verse 7 a man brings forth places, because Cush, Seba and Havilah are places, not people. And verse 13 has *îm* endings again; peoples are bringing forth peoples rather than individuals bringing forth individuals. Verse 15 indicates a man bringing forth a place. Finally, in verses 16-18 we are told that the various tribes, the Jebusites, the Amorites, the Gergasites, etc. came from one man—Canaan. Even though some individuals are named here, and not all are tribes, it certainly seems to me that to take these genealogies as chronology misses the mark.

The Generations of the Sons of Noah

In Genesis 10:1 we turn again to the literary form *these are the generations of,* this time in relationship to the sons of Noah: "Now these are the generations of the sons of Noah, Shem, Ham, and Japheth: and unto them were sons born after the flood." Beginning with verse 2, again the unimportant is dealt with first and quickly—with sufficient, true propositional truth—but quickly. Then the record turns to the more important line, Shem's, that flows on throughout the rest of the Bible.

We have seen that the literary form *these are the genera-*
156 *tions of* runs through the entire book of Genesis and

makes it a complete unit. Therefore, to treat the book of Genesis as less than a literary unit, to divide Genesis into two halves and read the two halves differently, is totally arbitrary. The only way to escape this is to say that the phrases *these are the generations of* were added by a final redactor (editor) as some of the documentarian higher critics do. But this argument rests on subjective decisions based on naturalistic presuppositions; it demands a final redactor who puts things in an order which fits their theories, their naturalistic position. Here the theory generates the data. The redactor would not be necessary if the weakness of their theory did not require him.

We have just spoken of the second literary form that emphasizes this same thing; namely, that throughout the whole book of Genesis, the factors not central to the main purpose of the book are dealt with first and quickly, and then the record returns to the central theme and treats it at length. These two literary forms together mean that we should approach the whole of Genesis with the expectation that the whole is to be read in the same way, from the first chapter to the last, before and after the time of Abraham. It could properly be said that these two factors make Genesis one of the most unified books in the Bible. In the light of this, anyone desiring to read parts of Genesis with a different form must give a clear reason why he does so. The witness of the New Testament makes this doubly certain: In every one of its references to any part of Genesis it takes the material to be normal space-time history, down to the small data. It always deals with the events in normal, straightforward, literary form.

We come in Genesis 10:21 and 11:10 to the line of Shem, because his is the important line. At 10:25 we read: "And unto Eber were born two sons: the name of the one was Peleg; for in his days was the earth divided." This may locate for us in the line of Shem the time when the divi- **157** sion at the tower of Babel took place. Verse 32 sums up the flow lines from the three sons of Noah: "These are the families of the sons of Noah, after their generations, in their nations: and by these were the nations divided in the earth after the flood." This verse and Genesis 9:19 indicate that the entire human race as it now stands came specifically from the three sons of Noah.

Babel

The next stage in the flow of history is an interesting and important event. It occurs in a place that is clearly delineated—the land of Shinar which is Babylonia in its widest sense. Genesis 11:1 reads: "And the whole earth was of one language, and of one speech." In the flow of history language was one. There was a common language among the descendants of Noah.

This isn't surprising, considering the tenacity with which men hold onto language. In Switzerland, for example, there are four languages and there is a language group clinging firmly to each one. Within one of them, the Romansh, there are about 60,000 people speaking two dialects, and this situation could continue practically forever. Therefore, that men with a common origin are speaking one language is to be expected.

Verse 4 makes what might be called the first public declaration of humanism: "And they said, Go to, let us build us a city and a tower, whose top may reach unto heaven; and let us make us a name, lest we be scattered abroad upon the face of the whole earth." We have already found this sort of humanism in the family of Cain, but what a strong humanistic statement this is! *Let's make a name for ourselves* so that *we* can maintain a human unity and *we* can achieve social stability.

In verse 7 God acts into this situation: "Come, let us [note the communication among members of the Trinity]

158

go down, and there confound their language, that they may not understand one another's speech" (ASV). The basic confusion among people is expressly stated to be language—not the color of skin, not race, not nation. Language is the key to the divisions of the peoples of the world.

The Bible indicates here, as it does constantly in the early chapters of Genesis, that all of the divisions of the whole world are a result of sin and the righteous judgment of God. Men said, Let us make a name for ourselves lest we be scattered, and then as a result of this attempt to make a unity on their own basis, "the LORD scattered them abroad from thence upon the face of all the earth" (v. 8). And this he did on the basis of their own speech.

Thus another division has emerged—not just one between man and God, man and himself, man and man, man and nature and nature and nature, but also between the men of the earth in their nations with implications that reach out into racial and cultural divisions, linked to linguistic differences. And all of them are rooted in the same source—the sin of man. Here at the tower, and always, man seeks to be autonomous.

The word *Babel* is interesting because it is given two different meanings. Genesis 11:9 says: "Therefore is the name of it called Babel; because the LORD did there confound the language of all the earth." In Hebrew the word *Babel* means confusion. The Babylonians themselves used the word to mean "the gate of God." So the Babylonians said, "We are the gate of God," and the Jews said, "No, you are confusion." Throughout Scripture, right up to the book of Revelation, the concept of Babylon stands crucial, Babylon saying, "We are the gate of God," and the Bible answering, "No, this is the place where the basic confusion of language occurred. You are confusion." Our own word *Babylon* is simply the word *Babel* with a Greek ending. **159**

The Generations of Shem

Genesis 11:10 takes up the generations of Shem as the Bible carries us still further along in the general flow of history. Here again we need to deal with the problem of genealogy and chronology. There are a number of things to notice.

First, in the Septuagint (the Greek translation of the Old Testament dating before the time of Christ) an extra name (Kainan) is recorded in verse 12. Kainan is stated to have lived 130 years, the phraseology fitting into exactly the same form as the other names. The intriguing thing (this is purely speculative) is that if this name does belong here, then this genealogy contains ten steps, the same number as the genealogy of the prediluvians in Genesis 5. One wonders, therefore, if this is a parallel to the genealogy of Christ in Matthew 1, where names are left out and then it is stated that there are fourteen generations from Abraham to David, and fourteen generations from David to Babylonian captivity, and fourteen generations from the Babylonian captivity to Christ (Mt. 1:17).

People often ask how Genesis 11:10 ff could not be a chronology with all the detail it contains, for example, in verses 12-13: "And Arphaxad lived five and thirty years, and begat Salah: And Arphaxed lived after he begat Salah four hundred and three years, and begat sons and daughters."

In Matthew 1:8, as I have pointed out, there is a tremendous jump in the genealogy. There could have been no mistake involved in making this jump, because the people who recorded these things knew the genealogies very well. Matthew 1:8 reads: "And Asa begat Jehoshaphat; and Jehoshaphat begat Joram; and Joram begat Uzziah" (ASV). But we saw, by comparing this to 1 Chronicles 3:11-12, that Uzziah's father, grandfather, and great-grand-father are omitted in Matthew's genealogy. So there is a lengthy break here. Therefore, what this passage in Matthew is really saying is: When Joram was a certain unnamed number of years old, be begat *someone who led to* Uzziah. And then, after Joram begat that unnamed individual, Joram lived a certain number of years and died.

But for the sake of the illustration let's be a little more imaginative and read it like this: "When Joram was 30 years old, he begat *someone who led to* Uzziah, and then Joram lived a certain number of years, had other children, and died." That is what this portion of Matthew 1:8 means. It does not state the number of years, but it does give us the form. And this is precisely the form we find throughout Genesis 11. In other words, the word *begat* in Genesis 11 does not require a first-generation father-son relationship. It can mean, *fathered someone who led to.* Adding this phrase to the genealogy in Genesis 11 would not change the situation at all. For example, if you added such a phrase to Genesis 11:14-15, then you would have exactly the same situation as in Matthew 1:8, because it would simply say that Salah begat *someone who led to* Eber. That is precisely what Matthew 1:8 says about Joram and Uzziah. Consequently there is no reason to let Genesis 11 change our conclusion that the genealogies do not constitute a chronology.

People have asked why the details are added. The best answer that has been given, I think, is simply that they form a parallel with the prediluvians where the ending of the form was *and he died.* The present passage doesn't say *and he died,* but it seems to involve the same mentality. The details are given, *and he lived so many years,* and then of course he died. The important names were the ones that were given, for they show the line.

When we realize that these genealogies give no guidance as to dating, we can understand why Professor B. B. Warfield said, "It is to theology, as such, a matter of entire indifference how long man has existed on earth."

In the flow of history in Genesis 1—11, therefore, I feel there really is no final discussion possible concerning dating. On the Bible's side there are the questions we've just considered, and on modern science's side there are certainly many questions as to whether science's dating systems are accurate. As I said in regard to the use of the Hebrew word *day* in Genesis 1, it is not that we have to accept the concept of the long periods of time modern science postulates, but rather that there are really no clearly defined terms upon which at this time to base a final debate.

The First Correlation with Secular History
In Genesis 11:26 we come to an entirely new situation because here there is a reference to the man Abraham to whom we can assign a specific date. We move from biblical history that is not open to correlation with secular history to biblical history that is open to such correlation. This does not imply that what has preceded is any less historic than what is recorded from this point on. But with Abraham we can assign an approximate date—2,000 B. C.

In Genesis 11:28 we are told that Abraham came from Ur of the Chaldees. We know a good deal about Ur of the Chaldees at the time when Abraham lived there and before because of the excavation that was done by Sir Charles Leonard Woolley in 1922 and 1934. We know, for example, that these people worshipped the moon goddess, but that they were far advanced in civilization and culture. Abraham was not just some strange wanderer, a Bedouin from the back side of the desert who didn't know anything. The excavations show us that the houses were made of brick and were whitewashed for aesthetic purposes. They stood two storied high. In the larger houses there were up to ten to twenty rooms. They had wonderfully equipped kitchens, a good plumbing system and sanitation. From the evidence that has been found, some people have thought that perhaps they taught cube root in their schools. The University of Pennsylvania has a cup dating two centuries before the time of Abraham that shows the magnificent workmanship these men were capable of. This cup is so marvelously made that no one today can surpass it, and it indicates the luxury of that place. Woolley's excavation volumes covering the Royal Tombs show pictures of the same marvelous work in gold and in alabaster as well.

In Genesis 12:1-3 we read: "Now the LORD had said unto Abram, Get thee out of thy country [that is, from this highly cultured place], and from thy kindred, and from thy father's house, unto a land that I will shew thee. And I will make of thee a great nation, and I will bless thee, and make thy name great; and thou shalt be a blessing: . . . and in thee shall all families of the earth be blessed." The Apostle Paul in his letter to the Galatians quotes from this section of Genesis and carefully ties what he is saying into the promise given there: "Even as Abraham believed God, and it was accounted to him for righteousness. Know ye therefore that they which are of faith, the same are the children of Abraham. And the Scripture, foreseeing that God would justify the heathen through faith, preached before the gospel unto Abraham, saying, In thee shall all nations be blessed. So then they which be of faith are blessed with faithful Abraham" (Gal. 3:6-9).

The promises of God, reaching back to Genesis 3:15, are coming by the time of Abraham into an even more clearly delineated area. The solution, which will be appropriate to the real dilemma of man and will take care of the consequence of guilt before a holy God who exists, will come through Abraham. After Abraham the flow of history goes on, and the promise through the Old Testament continues to become clearer. We come finally to that last prophet of **163** the Old Testament line, John the Baptist, who, when Jesus came and the moment of fulfillment was at hand, said, "Behold the Lamb of God, which taketh away the sin of the world" (Jn. 1:29).

The Flow of History: The Significance of Man

Thus the flow of history continues. History comes from someplace. History is going someplace. We are not born without a background. And there is a solution to the dilemma of man in the midst of history. What a contrast to modern man who has come to the awful conclusion that history isn't headed anywhere simply because he doesn't know that the history in Genesis 1–11 is true! But that goes for all of us. We too must listen, if we are to understand.

Many events happened before we were born and many others that we cannot remember occurred in our early life. If we are to know about them, our parents or others must tell us. A multitude of things which occurred before my time and are personally important to me I must learn from others. History is involved—things which really happened but which I must be told by another. It is exactly the same with the whole human race.

Historical knowledge is extending back further and further as we find older writing and as our excavations and our understanding of the artifacts increases. Secular history can tell us much about our past as a human race, and therefore our own place in it. But no matter how much writing we turn up and translate, no matter how many excavations we make and how many artifacts we study, secular history has not unearthed a clue to help explain the final "why" of what we find.

All the way back to the dawn of our studies we find man still being man. Wherever we turn—to the caves in the Pyrenees, to the Sumerians, and further back to the Neanderthal man burying his dead in flower petals—it makes no difference: Everywhere men show by their art and their acts that they observed themselves to be unique. And they were unique, unique as men in the midst of non-men. And yet they were as flawed with the dilemma of man, divisions of all kinds, as we are today.

So, just as a child needs to be told something of his personal history, mankind needs to be told of its history. Unless we are told about our beginnings, which secular study cannot trace, we cannot make sense of our present history. Twentieth-century man is looking at something— himself and the facts of history. He knows that something is really there, but he doesn't know what. This is exactly what Genesis 1–11 tells him. These chapters give the history which comes before anything secular historians have been able to ascertain, and it is that pre-secular history which gives meaning to man's present history. Imagine a little child who hasn't yet been told that he is indeed the legitimate heir to the throne. He lives in pauper's rags. Then somebody comes and tells him his previous history and he takes his rightful place. It is exactly this that we need. And it is exactly this that the history of Genesis 1–11 gives. It sets in perspective all the history we now have in our secular study.

Some people assume that one can spiritualize the history of the first eleven chapters of Genesis and it will make no difference. They assume that they can weaken the propositional nature of these chapters where they speak of history and the cosmos, and that nothing will change. But everything changes. These chapters tell us the "why" of all history man knows through his studies, including the "why" of each man's personal history. For this, Genesis 1–11 is more important than anything else one could have.

In these chapters we learn of the historic, space-time **165** creation out of nothing; the creation of man in God's image; a real, historic, space-time, moral Fall; and the understanding of the present abnormality in the divisions that exist between God and man, man and himself, man and man, man and nature and nature and nature. These chapters also tell us the flow of the promise God made from the beginning concerning the solution to these divisions. This is what Genesis 1–11 gives us, and it is climactic. Naturalistic, rationalistic history only sees the results. If I am to understand the world as it is and myself as I am, I must know the flow of history given in these chapters. Take this away, and the flow of the rest of history collapses.

If a man attributes a wrong cause to the dilemma and divisions of men, he will never come up with the right answer no matter how good a will he has. Man as he stands since the Fall is not normal, and consequently the solution must be appropriate to what we know to be the cause of his problems and his dilemma. A mere physical solution is inadequate, because man's dilemma is not physical. Nor can it be metaphysical, because the problem of man, as we know it in Genesis 1–11, is not primarily metaphysical. The problem of man is moral, for by choice he stands in rebellion against God. And any appropriate solution must fill this moral need.

He who is the seed of the woman has bruised the serpent's head. But what good is that to us if we will not listen? If we won't listen, we won't understand.

appendix

footnotes

Over the last few years my wife Edith and I have been carrying through a somewhat comprehensive program of writing. This book is one of the pieces.

My first two books were *The God Who Is There* and *Escape from Reason*. Wrongly—perhaps because it was shorter—many people have assumed that *Escape from Reason* is the "introduction" and *The God Who Is There* a development of it. In fact, the opposite is the truth. *The God Who Is There* was written first; it lays the groundwork, establishes the terminology and sets out the basic thesis. We at L'Abri have attempted to show that Christianity has balance: that biblical exegesis gives intellectual depth, and also, in the area of practical living and beauty, Christianity has a relation to the whole man. Beginning with the Christian system as God has given it to men in the verbalized propositional revelation of the Bible, one can move along and find that every area of life is touched by truth and a song. *Escape from Reason* works out this principle particularly in the philosophical area of Nature and Grace, and shows how modern culture has grown from polluted roots far back in the late Middle Ages.

After these two books perhaps *He Is There and He Is Not Silent* should have been published. That would have been its logical place. The three make a unified base; without them the various applications in the other books are **169** really suspended in space. *He Is There and He Is Not Silent* deals with one of the most fundamental of all questions: how we know, and how we know we know. Unless our epistemology is right, everything is going to be wrong. That is why it goes with *The God Who Is There*—a link emphasized by its title. The infinite-personal God is there, but also he is not silent and that changes the whole world.

On the base of these three books, which constitute a conscious unity (a unity which I believe rests on the unity of Scripture itself), all the other books which have come or will come depend. They apply this unified Christian system to various areas. It should be noted that *The God Who Is There* has two appendices which deal with two specific problems: the middle-class church in the twentieth century and the practice of truth in Christian work and evangelism. These are developed in the later books. *Death in the City* is exegetical, picking up the application of the earlier books to American and Northern European culture as it has turned away from what God has given us as a base.

Next came *Pollution and the Death of Man,* the Christian answer to the ecological dilemma, based on the same consistent system. *The Church at the End of the 20th Century* moved into other areas of application—sociology and ecclesiology. The two appendices to that book, *Adultery and Apostasy* and *The Mark of the Christian* (also published as a separate small book) picked up the theme touched on in the second appendix to *The God Who Is There*: They emphasize the balance to be struck between the practice of the purity of the visible church and the love which ought to mark relationships between all true Christians, no matter what their differences over secondary matters are. There is also a fuller and practical treatment of ecclesiology in *The Church before the Watching World.*

It might be alleged that this is merely a new, arid scholasticism, applied in the areas of epistemology, ecclesiology, ecology, sociology and so forth. If it were, then it would be nothing but a tinkling cymbal. Three books, however, redress the balance. The last chapter of *Death in the City*, "The Universe and Two Chairs," is important here. Edith's book, *L'Abri*, is a vital element, and without it the other books lack true unity and balance. Her book shows how acting upon the fact that the infinite-personal God is really there has worked out in day-by-day practice in the community of L'Abri. *True Spirituality* is likewise crucial; it is a systematic treatment of the whole basis of a Christian's living in an open relationship with God and then with himself and others. Edith's book *Hidden Art* has an important place as it carries these matters into the practical and beautiful area of creativity in the Christian's life. The present book on the first eleven chapters of Genesis fits into the whole structure by giving a more fully developed exegetical base to the decisive point of beginnings.

Taken together, all of these books represent a unified concept which was developed over many years of study and many years of experiential knowledge of our God who is there.

footnotes

Chapter One

[1] For a much more full treatment of the material in the next few paragraphs see *He Is There and He Is Not Silent* (Tyndale House Publishers, 1972).

[2] See *Back to Freedom and Dignity* (InterVarsity Press, 1972), in which I deal with B. F. Skinner's book, *Beyond Freedom and Dignity* (New York: Alfred A. Knopf, 1971).

[3] The biblical teaching concerning the Trinity is, of course, developed more fully in the New Testament, but for other indications of the Trinity in the Old Testament see Gen. 11:7; Is. 6:8; 44:6; and 48:16.

[4] The Greek aorist is a once-for-all past tense.

[5] This verse is sometimes used by those who say faith itself gives knowledge and thus undercuts the necessity of the content of Scripture. However, it is Scripture which gives the knowledge that is referred to here, and then we, on the basis of what the Bible claims is sufficient reason, believe what God has told us in the Bible.

Chapter Two

[1] There may be a difference between the methodology by which we gain knowledge from what God tells us in the Bible and the methodology by which we gain it from scientific study, but this does not lead to a dichotomy as to the facts. In practice it may not always be possible to correlate the two studies because of the special situation involved, yet if both studies can be adequately pursued, there will be no final conflict. For example, the Tower of Babel: whether we come at it from biblical knowledge given by God or by scientific study, either way when we are done with our study, the Tower of Babel was either there or it was not there. The same thing is true of Adam. Whether we begin with the conceptual apparatus of

archaeology and anthropology or whether we begin with the knowledge given us in the Bible, if it were within the realm of science's knowledge to do so, in both cases we would end with knowledge about Adam's bones. Science by its natural limitations cannot know all we know from God in the Bible, but in those cases where science can know, both sources of knowledge arrive at the same point, even if the knowledge is expressed in different terms. And it is important to keep in mind that there is a great difference between saying the same thing in two different symbol systems and actually saying two different exclusive things but hiding the difference with the two symbol systems. What the Bible teaches where it touches history and the cosmos and what science teaches where it touches the same areas do not stand in a discontinuity. There indeed must be a place for the study of general revelation (the universe and its form, and man with his mannishness), that is, a place for true science. But on the other side, it must be understood that there is no automatic need to accommodate the Bible to the statements of science. There is a tendency for some who are Christians and scientists to always place special revelation (the teaching of the Bible) under the control of general revelation and science, and never or rarely to place general revelation and what science teaches under the control of the Bible's teaching. That is, though they think of that which the Bible teaches as true and that which science teaches as true, in reality they tend to end with the truth of science as more true than the truth of the Bible.

[2] In the earlier passages, up to chapter 5, the word *Adam* is used with a definite article referring to a specific man. In Genesis 5:1-2 it is used without the article and thus seems better translated as *mankind*.

Chapter Five

[1] Words have become so devalued today that we often have to use cumbersome terms to make what we mean understood. The word *fact* does not necessarily mean anything anymore. *Fact* can just mean upper-story religious truth, and therefore we have to use an awkward term like *brute fact*. In this particular case, we are fortunate because the liberal theologians themselves use the term *brute fact* for what they *don't mean* by facts. The historic Fall is not an interpretation: It is a *brute fact*. There is no room for hermeneutics here, if by hermeneutics we mean explaining away the *brute factness* of the Fall. That there was a Fall is not an upper-story statement— **173**

that is, it is not *in this sense* a "theological" or "religious" statement. Rather, it is a historic, space-time, *brute-fact,* propositional statement. There was time, space-time history, before the Fall, and then man turned from his proper integration point by choice, and in so doing there was *moral* discontinuity; man became abnormal.

In speaking of *facts* and *brute facts,* we are speaking of facts in the space-time sense, that which is open to the normal means of verification and falsification. As I stress in the Appendix to *The Church before the Watching World,* this does *not* mean they are then to be taken as sterile facts. These biblical facts are facts in past history, but they have, and should have, meaning in our present existential, moment-by-moment lives.

Furthermore, in speaking of the Bible's statements as propositional truth we are *not* saying that all communication is on the level of mathematical formula. There can be other levels (for example, figures of speech or the special force of poetry); but there is a *continuity*—a unity not a *discontinuity*—between these "other levels" and a flow of propositions given in normal syntax and using words in their normal definition, and this is a continuity which reason can deal with. Take an example outside of the Bible: Shakespeare's communication with his figures of speech is a much richer human communication than is mere mathematical formula. The "other levels" (for example, his figures of speech) add enrichment. Yet, if, as in far-out modern prose and poetry, there are only, or almost only, figures of speech, with no adequate running continuity that can be stated in propositional form using normal syntax and words with normal meanings, no one knows what is being said. As a matter of fact, some modern writers and artists deliberately work this way so that this will be the case. Their work becomes only a quarry for subjective experiences and interpretations inside of the head of the reader or viewer. The early chapters of Genesis quickly come to this place if they are read other than as in propositional form using normal syntax and words in their normal meaning. As an example, Paramhansa Yogananda did this in his book *Autobiography of a Yogi* and most easily turned these chapters into a powerful Hindu tract.

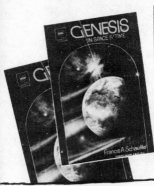